D0917120

Adolf Olson
2387 Childrabe Ave:
St Paul, Minn

MODERN SPIRITISM

MODERN SPIRITISM

ITS SCIENCE AND RELIGION

BY

A. T. SCHOFIELD, M.D.

Vice-President Victoria Institute, &c., &c.

Author of
"The Unconscious Mind,"
"Borderlands of Science,"
"The Goal of the Race"

Πνεῦμα ἕτερον λαμβάνετε ὃ οὐκ ἐκρύξαμεν.

AUTHORIZED AMERICAN EDITION

WITH A FOREWORD
BY
NEWELL DWIGHT HILLIS
Pastor of Plymouth Church.

PHILADELPHIA
P. BLAKISTON'S SON & CO.
1012 WALNUT STREET
1920

PREFACE

MODERN custom doubtless suggests that it would be well that a book like this, by an author who has not hitherto written on the subject, should be commended to its readers by a "Foreword" from some well-known authority.

The author may be pardoned if he very briefly states why this preface is written; and, in doing so, he would also recommend that it be read *before* the book, and not, as is now so common, afterwards.

Even previously to entering on a medical career the author began to study psychological problems, with the result that many years ago he wrote the first English book on "The Unconscious Mind." A paper he read on the subject at the Harveian Society was received with howls of derision, and the authorities were rebuked for allowing it to offend the ears of its learned members; all of which shows to our wiser generation the archaic condition of the psychology of that day. It is true I do not regard the unconscious mind as cosmic, as is the subliminal mind of F. W. H. Myers, and to a large extent the subconscious mind of Thomas Jay Hudson, of America; but substantially it is the same.

Professor William James has written scathingly of what was the condition then of psychological science for want of this knowledge.

Once it is recognised that consciousness is not co-extensive with mind, but only reaches less than half the way, it can be readily conceived that the word "subconscious" is the best for that mental region which can at times be brought within the range of consciousness by forced introspection; while "unconscious" is a far better word for that part which never by any effort can be brought within consciousness. If consciousness be called the "eye" of the mind it clears our thoughts, for much exists psychically that is beyond mental vision.

When the reader grasps the fact that the most modern views of Spiritist psychical phenomena show that the medium's trance is very largely, at any rate, a condition of unconscious mental activity, with more or less complete abeyance of consciousness, the relevancy of the above statement to our subject will be readily admitted.

Psychological problems have indeed for over thirty years been to me an absorbing study, including all those connected with Spiritism, many of which, I freely confess, are not yet fully solved.

Borderland questions have always proved a great attraction, and what I call the true Spiritualism of the Divine Revelation has long provided for me what I have ever felt to be the most elevated study of which the human mind is capable.

This book has been written at the very special and earnest request of a friend well known in the medical world, whose views as to the urgency of presenting to the public some fairly comprehensive monograph on the subject at this time coincided with my own.

The recent accession to the ranks of this doubtful cult of such well-known and honoured names as Sir Oliver Lodge and Sir A. Conan Doyle has undoubtedly acted as a stimulus to Spiritism.

A more critical view, however, of their work, as given towards the close of this book, seems to throw some doubt on the value of their accession to the deeper interests of this new "Religion."

It is most unfortunate for its success that Spiritism seeks to be both a science and a religion, which is impossible. So long as Sir Oliver Lodge was content to be scientific, which, in this connection, was but a very short time, so long did he advance the scientific status of Spiritism. But when he propounded dogmas, and when Sir A. Conan Doyle asserted *tout court* that "Spiritism *is* a religion," science was arrayed against both; and Sir William Barrett, in his earnest attempts to confine its objects to scientific investigations, was defeated.

Its present condition is, therefore, undoubtedly chaotic, and the benefit, or otherwise, that it derives from its recent distinguished converts will depend, in the author's estimation, entirely on the light in which one regards Spiritism: whether that in which Sir William Barrett sees it, or that in which it seems to fascinate Sir A. Conan Doyle.

Thirdly, and lastly, to round off this lay sermon, I have been studying for many years what may without offence be termed borderland disease, that is, those conditions which are somewhat casually included under the vague term of "functional nerve disorders." Here conditions allied to the trances of mediums are by no means rare, and their

continuous study over so long a period has certainly
evolved an amount of analytical power in dealing
with them that is not inherent. All this has helped
me now. While I have not disguised my own beliefs,
I am in hopes that some at least of my readers will
admit that I have presented the case for and against
Spiritism fairly and squarely. If Spiritism were all
fraud, it would be no real danger to the nation; it
is because it is not that this book is written. My
work is to show that, however bad fraud may be,
the actual action of evil spirits is infinitely worse.
The subject on which I have been most dogmatic, is
the one point on which I find myself in full agreement
with the leading Spiritists—and that is its great
hidden dangers.

I am glad this book appears after the Great War,
and not before, for amidst its many evils the war
has at least done one good. It has made the simple,
the straightforward, the true, of greater value than
formerly, and men to-day are not likely to accept
the claims of Spiritism, however endorsed, without
full investigation.

All the author asks, therefore, is that the book
be read in such a spirit and without prejudice,
for he then believes it probable that his readers
can come to no other conclusion than that at which
he himself has arrived.

ALFRED T. SCHOFIELD, M.D.

10, HARLEY STREET,
LONDON.

FOREWORD

Cicero's question, "Is there a meeting place of the dead?" asked two thousand years ago, has suddenly taken on new meanings. The death of his daughter, Tullia, filled the heart of the great Roman lawyer with acute anguish. He read Socrates' arguments for the immortal hope over and over again, but with an increasing feeling that the argument was incomplete. Now comes a moment when three millions of homes in Britain, France and the United States have lost the noble boy whose future before that day of battle held only high hopes for all who loved the young soldier. Many a father and mother and lover have coerced the lips into silence, and with a solemn pride oft exclaimed, "God's soldier let him be! I could not wish him to a fairer death!" And then comes a revulsion, with the awful sense of loneliness, and the emptiness of life.

The inevitable result of the world war, therefore, and of the hillsides of Belgium and France, billowy with the graves of the noble dead, was a revival of spiritualism. Everywhere men are saying, "Does the soul survive bodily death?" Is immortality the next step in the ascending progress of the soul? Is it true that there is an unseen realm, within the reach of an outstretched arm? Since without the optic nerve there is no summer's landscape, is it possible that most of us have no spiritual nerve toward the realm immortal, while now and then an occasional person with a clairvoyant sense receives hints of an unseen world? Suddenly, scientists are answering the question in the affirmative. Maeterlinck, Conan Doyle, Sir Oliver Lodge, and thousands of others insist that death does not end all. The arguments based upon instinct, the ascent of man, and the principles of philosophers, have reinforced the teachings and experience of Jesus for multitudes who hold to the Christian faith. Meanwhile, the spiritualist has come to the front. It is said that the number of persons who attended spiritualistic meetings on a single memorial Sunday, equalled the number of those that attended the Christian churches in the city of London on the self-same day. Even though we question the accuracy of this estimate it still remains true that uncounted multitudes are interested in the ouija board, in spirit photography, in seances, and in mediums, who claim to speak while in a trance, and to be voicing a message from the dead. It has, therefore, become important to the last degree that the scientist and the experts in physiological psychology, and the students of nervous phenomena should analyze this mass of material, sift the wheat from the chaff, prick the bubbles that have been blown by enthusiasts, and spread out before the normal mind the few facts that are left. Dr. Schofield's book represents the patient, long-continued investigations of a man singularly gifted by nature and trained by long experience to distinguish between that which is seeming and that which is real. His volume has received a warm welcome from the most thoughtful people in Great Britain, and it deserves careful scrutiny of Americans who are interested in the border land, where the seen and the unseen meet and mingle.

NEWELL DWIGHT HILLIS.

CONTENTS

CONTENTS

CHAPTER I

INTRODUCTORY

THE GUILD OF THE SILVER FERN

A FEW years ago I got an invitation to attend a gathering of the members of the Guild of the Silver Fern, in order that I might tell them, as the herald in England of the unconscious mind,* whether the voices which they, as Spiritists,† heard were *subjective*, *i.e.*, from themselves, or *objective*, that is, from some other agency.

The Unconscious Mind

Most of my readers will at least have heard of F. W. H. Myers, Vice-president of the Psychical Research Society, even if they have not read his great book on "Human Personality."‡ In this, at considerable length, he explains what he calls "subliminal consciousness," or consciousness "below the threshold," *i.e.*, below the cognizance of our ordinary consciousness—in other words, an unconscious consciousness; and this, I gather, he believes is in each person a part of what he calls a great cosmic mind.

---

* "The Unconscious Mind," A. T. Schofield, M.D. Hodder and Stoughton. 1898.

† Modern and short term for Spiritualists.

‡ He is the author also of that unique poem "St. Paul."

Now a "consciousness" of which I am unconscious is, in relation to myself, unconsciousness;
hence *my* term "the unconscious mind," which I
much prefer to "subliminal," or "sub-conscious."
It seems to me that we have but one mind (I know
of no cosmic mind, other than God Himself) which,
however, in us exists in three conditions.

Regarding consciousness as "*the eye of the mind*,"
by which we can see mental processes, and comparing
the mind as a whole to an island, I would regard the
first mental condition of *full consciousness* as comparable to that part of the island which is always
above water. The *second* condition of *sub-consciousness* I would describe as that part of the island
which is sometimes visible and sometimes invisible
according to the state of the tide. In us this represents that part of our mentality which can be
brought into consciousness by strong introspection,
but which is usually outside it.

The *third* condition of *unconsciousness* (Myers'
subliminal consciousness) is the rest of the island
under water, which is always invisible. To me, as
I think I have demonstrated,* the mental processes
that are wholly unseen by the eye of consciousness
are just as truly psychic and purposive as those that
we see and know. The fact of their being unseen
does not, as so many seem to think, make them either
unreal or non-mental.

This is, perhaps, a long enough digression to make
what follows intelligible.

*"The Unconscious Mind."

Meeting of the Guild

I found myself in the evening in a large double drawing-room in the south-western district of London, some sixty or seventy of the Guild being present, including some well-known Spiritists, and a few others distinguished as pioneers in Psychic Research and in Theosophy. I was at once asked to open the discussion on the subject—"Whether the voices heard by mediums, or the messages received through the various media of movements, tappings, and automatic writing were *subjective*— the product conscious or unconscious of human beings in the room—or of some other force outside themselves, and, therefore, *objective*."

I said that I should much prefer to hear the views of experts in Spiritism first upon the subject, and that, if they would kindly open the discussion, I would speak later on. This was agreed to, and many views were advanced; and by far the majority were in favour of spirit communications being mainly from some other spirit than the medium's, though I was surprised to find the subjective view was also in favour, and was ably supported. When I rose to speak and looked round upon my audience, and considered the Quest upon which they were embarked, as old speakers used to say, "my spirit was stirred within me," and I asked permission to make a few general remarks before entering on the important subject of the evening.

The Great Spirit World

I said, in effect, that I felt sure we all agreed that, in the abstract, Spiritism, or at any rate

1—2

Spiritualism, was the highest and noblest study that could engage the thoughts of mankind. In its true meaning it is to seek to know and understand the Father of spirits; it is to seek to know and understand the real, the true, the invisible, the eternal; for all that we know, all that is obvious— the material and physical—are not the real, and the things that are seen are temporal.

Not only so, but God is a spirit, and in the Bible we are told that St. Paul, discoursing on Mars' Hill to the philosophers of Athens, desired that men should "seek God, if haply they might feel after Him, and find Him, though He is not far from each one of us." Here the real object of true Spiritualism is shown and enjoined; and we ask fearlessly, Can anything be nobler or more Divine than such a quest? I think not.

'But, alas! when we turn from this, and consider what so-called Modern Spiritism has become to-day in the midst of great Christian nations, we may well ask if we have not succeeded in degrading this Spiritual Cult almost beyond recognition. The difference in the concept between the words "Spiritism" and "Spiritual" to-day is only comparable, to a Christian mind, to that between "Jesuit" and "Jesus." Without any offence to Catholics, all will agree as to the contrast of the concept.

Evil Associations of Spiritism

'Is there in this company one Spiritist who has not recoiled with, at least, disgust from the puerile pranks, too often steeped in falsehood and deception, that so frequently characterise their meetings, and have so degraded the very name of Spiritism? And what has been the result? What is the net outcome of the Quest so far? Has one single noble, or lofty, or divine thought been added to our previous concepts? On the other hand, have we not been brought into the closest and most undesired contact with deception and fraud of an undoubted character; and too often, one regrets to say, with evil, malice, and sometimes, as Mr. Sinnet has testified, of unspeakable corruption? One is brought into touch in Modern Spiritism with a world of which one had no previous concept, of a most undesirable nature, which has perhaps been best described by Maeterlinck in his "Unknown Guest."

'It is true that indirectly an unseen spirit world has thus been revealed and demonstrated to many who utterly denied it before; but the net result of Spiritism so far is most disappointing, to say nothing of its undoubted dangers to spirit, soul, and body; which, to their honour, leading Spiritists are among the first to point out.

Voices are Often Objective

'Turning now to the immediate question of the evening, as to whether the communications received by mediums, or other means, are subjective or purely objective, my reply is that some are undoubtedly objective, and that constantly at séances spirits other than our own manifest their presence.*

'Setting on one side for a moment those supposed

---

* I say this in spite of what I shall advance later on of the part played by our own unconscious mind.

communications which are produced by fraud, and those attributed, often erroneously, to telepathy and various forms of thought transference, there remains a certain number of purely objective utterances, surely the result of intelligences other than our own.*

'It does not, of course, in the least follow that such beings are desirable or helpful in any way; indeed, there is too much reason to believe that, in perhaps the majority of cases, they are distinctly injurious in many ways that I cannot now describe.

The Apotheosis of Spiritualism

'But in all this there is nothing new. Perhaps there are those present who do not attach any special authority to the Bible; but to the many who do, it will be a matter of great interest to recall that it represents God ever as the seeker after men. He not only cares for them in every possible way, but is always anxious to get into communication with them. What, indeed, is prayer (when viewed rightly, and not as a mere question of asking for favours), but a true spiritual séance in the highest sense? Are not these well-known lines illustrative of this as to prayer?—

'"Thither by faith we upward soar,
    Till time and sense are all no more,
  And Heaven comes down our souls to greet,
    And glory crowns the Mercy-seat."

'Such is nothing less than the apotheosis of true Spiritualism as divinely taught and enjoined.

* During the war there can be no doubt that there was a great increase in the subjective, that is, messages supposed to come from others which were really suggestions of the unconscious mind.

But in this aspect the messages from our world to the spirit world are more clear, as a rule, than the responses, which our dull ears are so slow to receive.

'Let us look at the subject from another point of view, which will, I think, give a full and clear answer to the question I have to answer.

The Rich Fool

'Those who are familiar with the Bible will remember the parable of "the rich farmer," or, as some have it, "the rich fool," for he was, indeed, both. For any who cannot recall it, I may say the story told by our Lord Christ is that of a rare phenomenon in these days—a contented farmer; and the reason of his state of mind was not far to seek. His "ground brought forth plentifully," and as he stood in his farmyard he was much perplexed, for he saw at once his buildings were not half large enough to hold such a bounteous harvest. So, being a provident man with an eye to the future, he at once faced the problem of insufficient "stedding." Looking around his barns he planned it all out (you can see him doing it), and the look of perplexity gradually changes into one of satisfaction as he sees his way out.

' "This barn must be pulled down and a much larger one erected; another should be greatly lengthened; additional ones should be built in spare corners." So far, so good; no trace of any foolishness, but the very reverse—wise foresight. The foolishness comes when he begins to speak to his soul. Like many others, on the material plane he is all there; but on the spirit plane he is all abroad!

And this, not because his soul here means his "spirit," which it does not, but because of two cordinal errors. The one that his life, his ego, himself, can certainly look forward to many years of ease; whereas, as reminded elsewhere and every hour, we "know not what a day may bring forth." The other is that he wholly ignores the spirit life and its requirements. But all this only in passing. I hurry on to what follows: "But God said unto him, Thou foolish one, this night is thy soul required of thee."

'This marvellous drama is lost to us unless we understand the phenomena of inaudible voices, and of the true answer to the question concerning which we are gathered to-night.

Our Mediæval Bible

'I suppose no one in these rooms imagines the Almighty God, in some human form, or possibly some supernatural form, such as we commonly associate with angelic beings, appeared to this farmer?

'We must not forget to note here the curious fact, often overlooked, that the Bible we use is not in our language at all, but in the mediæval English of 300 years ago, now practically obsolete; with the result that not only is the true meaning frequently obscured, but that in reading it we find ourselves in a mediæval atmosphere, and absolutely out of touch with modern thought.* The result is that in studying the Bible we conjure up mediæval pictures,

---

* We often think this is due to the Bible itself; whereas it is largely on account of the mediæval English, as one soon finds who reads Dr. Weymouth's "Testament in Modern English."

and imagine here some such angelic visitation as is
recorded elsewhere.

How God Speaks

'The facts were probably far different, and much
simpler. The farmer, satisfied with his building
plans, and ready now for his supper, would turn
back towards the house in a complacent and contented frame of mind, and certainly not contem-
plating his own death. If one of us had at that
moment been standing at the farmhouse door, it is
not unlikely we should have seen something like the
following. The farmer, slowly approaching, would
suddenly halt in the middle of the path, and his
ruddy brown face become perceptibly whiter for a
moment; the colour would then return, and he
would resume his walk. When he reached the door,
you would probably comment on what you had seen,
and ask him, "Why did you stop just now in the
middle of the path? You looked as if you were
deep in thought." "Did I? was I?" he might reply,
in rather a dazed manner. "Oh yes, I remember,
as I was coming up the path a strange thought
struck me, 'Supposing I died to-night?' You see I
am just returning from the yard, where I have been
planning how to house my crops, and thinking I was
in for a good time for many years to come." "I
see, I see," the friend might reply.

A Thought Struck Me

' Probably it was in some such manner God
spoke then, as he speaks now, every day, to men.
I need not here dwell on the tragic *dénouements*

—the supper, the heavy sleep, the vain knocking on the door in the morning, the forcing of the lock, the scared faces, the still form, the hush of death as it is realised that the farmer has suddenly been called to his account from the midst of his prosperity. Here, then, is the solution of our problem. We, and not mediums only, *do* hear voices other than our own; and to do so it is by no means necessary, or even desirable, that we should have séances, or needful we should be professed Spiritists. Our common description of the voice of God by His Spirit is, "a thought *struck* me;" that is, we describe it in physical and objective terms. This is significant and most interesting.

'God is ever speaking objectively to men in dreams, in visions, and in thoughts that strike us. The Bible is not only itself the voice of God, as all Christians know, but this voice is constantly speaking to us in other ways, and is so represented in Scripture.*

A Noble Study

'If, then, the great Father of Spirits deigns thus to speak to His creatures, does it not seem to all of us that the highest and noblest vocation of true Spiritualism would be to study the differences between "I thought" and "a thought struck me;" between the subjective from our own unconscious mind and the objective from the spirit world. And, seeing that Christianity has revealed to us the two worlds of spirits, good and bad (the latter, at any rate, as many Spiritists will admit, amply confirmed by the

* A well-known evangelist told me that one-third of those he met ascribed their conversion to visions in dreams.

experiences of modern Spiritism), might not a further Quest be to seek the best means to become a true discerner of spirits, so as to be able to distinguish, first, between my own voice and another's, and, secondly, between the voices of good and evil spirits?'

I said a good deal more on the facts that these objective voices generally seem to speak from within —less frequently they are from without.*

Our Father in Heaven

If, as Scripture tells us, the bodies of Christians are indeed temples of the Holy Spirit, it is clear His dwelling-place is in the unconscious mind (F. W. H. Myers' subliminal mind), and this for a most obvious and necessary reason. If God dwelt inside us in the conscious mind, we could not fail ever to pay adoring worship, and to pray to the God within; whereas our prayer is to be addressed to "Our Father which *art in Heaven*," and we are practically unconscious of the amazing fact, dogmatically stated in the Bible, that all Christians, in virtue of the New Birth, have the Spirit of Christ dwelling in them. To me, and perhaps to many others, this is a wonderful proof, not only of the fact of the unconscious mind, but of the Divine wisdom in selecting a part of the mind outside our own consciousness for His dwelling-place. But these are all great subjects for study which I earnestly commend to every earnest student of spirit mysteries, for, I doubt not, the powers of the uncon-

* See "Another World, or the Fourth Dimension." D. Allen & Son, 40, Museum Street, W.C. Second edition.

scious mind can really solve many of the problems that perplex us.

Two Opposite Directions

I was agreeably surprised at the close of my words to find that many came up and thanked me for them in warm terms, while others equally warmly expressed their own views on Spiritism and its objects, which widely diverged from those I had suggested.

It did not take me long to find that, in this Spiritist Society of the Silver Fern, I was with two entirely different sets of people, with different objects and different destinations.

Many of my readers, waiting at an "island" platform at some railway station, where the "down" trains run at one side and the "up" trains in an opposite direction at the other, have noticed in the waiting passengers two distinct classes. If the "down" trains run to the seaside, and the "up" to town, the two elements in the crowd are clearly distinguishable. Though standing at the moment side by side, in five minutes they would be travelling in opposite directions, never probably to meet again. The importance in life is not where one may be found at any particular moment, but *in what direction he is travelling*. It was so in these drawing-rooms. One could clearly discern that, although all were together in the same society, they were there for two opposite reasons. To many the Silver Fern represented their farthest advance towards the light —the spiritual world, God, and Christianity. They had been either materialists or absolutely careless as to things unseen; but this society had succeeded in awakening in them a sense and a belief in another and a higher world, and possibly prepared their minds for an intelligent hearing and acceptance of Christianity. These would undoubtedly be regarded by Christians as travelling on the "up" lines.

On the Down Grade

The rest, and probably the majority, on the contrary, represented lapses from the Christian faith, and their presence that night their acceptance of modern Spiritism in its place. To believers, the shifting sands of the vague utterances of mediums seems but a poor and doubtful substitute on which to build one's faith, when compared with what Gladstone used to call "the impregnable rock of Holy Scripture." From a truly spiritual point of view, the same position in this society side by side represented, in the one case, the zenith, and, in the other, the nadir of their place with regard to Christianity; for, as I shall hope to show in this monograph, while there is much, very much, of interest in all researches into the unseen and unknown, the Spiritist faith, which, as we shall see is gradually being formulated into dogmas, contradicts categorically, point by point, all the fundamentals of Christianity.

True Spiritualism Wanted

One wonders sometimes if it is too much to hope for, that some day a true Spiritual quest may be established, not for necromancy, nor for the mountebank performances so common to-day, but for the serious and lofty object of learning more of the Father of Spirits, of the Holy Spirit and His action in connection with man, with other phenomena of the spirit world which everywhere surrounds us and are yet so imperfectly understood by Christians. All this, and much more, is still an unexplored region, and awaits some such concerted action as I have suggested.

There can be no doubt that Modern-Spiritism, with all its faults and follies, has done much towards promoting a general consensus that there *is* life after death, and a vast invisible spirit world; and so far has done service to man. More we cannot say, and we think in these pages it will be shown that much, alas! of its work is not only evil in itself, but full of mental and spiritual dangers of the gravest character, too often ending in the loss of reason, to say nothing of the actual physical dangers that beset it.

Christianity a Living Force

It will be noted that throughout this chapter I speak of Christianity as a still living force, and a living faith, and of the Bible as the Word of God, in spite of the bold, but most erroneous, assertions of most Spiritist writers that the old faith is dead and gone, and is held by no modern thinker. It is surprising to find the well-known method of Hæckel, of putting forward unproved ex-cathedra statements as well-known scientific facts, repeated by Spiritist men of science to-day, after the exposure of Hæckel's procedure in the "Riddle of the Universe." One has but for one moment to compare the leaders of modern Spiritism with the leading Christian men of the day to prove that Christianity is still a great and living force; and all advanced against it requires careful proof rather than irresponsible general statements and unproved assumptions. Personally I believe that never since the apostles' days have there been so many true evangelical Christians in the earth as in the present day all over the world, and never so many ready to die for the faith that is in them.

The Manual of True Spiritualism

We shall, therefore, continue to take Christianity as the faith of this country, and the Bible as the Word of God, and, in doing so, we come across an amazing truth, which I have already touched on. For Christianity is *the* spiritual faith, and the Bible *the* spiritual book. All that which is called by its leaders "Modern Spiritism" seeks to prove as to existence after death and another world, the Bible, from cover to cover, asserts as true, and is a commonplace to the humblest Christian. Not only so, but "where there is no vision, the people perish," and the Bible is full of spirit visions and spirit voices. Many of the familiar physical wonders of Spiritism are recorded, such as levitation—the swimming of the axe-head (2 Kings vi.); transportation from place to place, as in the case of Philip in the Acts; the shaking of rooms; the appearance of tongues of fire, and many others. Communications from the spirit world are (though not from the dead) the very essence of the Bible. In short, there is no book in the whole world to compare with the Word of God in making known the powers of the world invisible, and showing its profound influence on the whole destiny of man and in every stage of his earthly career.

Doubtless, the Bible is the greatest manual on true Spiritualism, stamped as it is with Divine authority, that exists; and, as we investigate the present position of Modern Spiritism, we shall find that between it and the true Bible-Spiritualism a great gulf is indeed fixed.

In Favour of Spiritual Research

Let us clearly understand that, so far from this book being written against researches into the spirit world, it protests solely and entirely against the degradation of this noble science by the Modern Spiritism of the day. So far from denying a future existence and another world, it takes its stand on both as Divine truths, only pointing out how transcendent are the Bible details concerning both when compared with Spiritist communications.

I shall also show that the stand the Bible takes against communication with another world, so far from being sweeping and general, is strictly confined to these degrading and dangerous practices so largely revived in Modern Spiritism, and the practice of necromancy.

All this must be always borne in mind while we carefully consider the practices and doctrines of Modern Spiritism from the utterances of its most distinguished leaders.

After a general survey of the subject, we shall consider first of all its claims as a Science, and then as a Religion.

CHAPTER II

THE HISTORY OF SPIRITISM

MODERN SPIRITISM is, according to its exponents, merely a new development, clothed in new words of a cult thousands of years old; one might have said, with equal truth, well-nigh as old as the human race.

In the *Encyclopædia Britannica* Spiritism is defined as "a belief that the spirit world manifests itself by producing in the physical world effects inexplicable by the known laws of nature"; but later, in the *Spiritist Magazine*, the definition is further developed as follows. Spiritism is defined as "a belief based on facts through a system of mediumship. Its cardinal truths being that of a world of spirits; and the continuity of the existence of the individual spirit through the momentary eclipse of death."*

* To this we may add the following from "The True Light," by G. G. André, F.G.S., A.M.I.C.E. (1907):—"What is this spiritism, and what is this theosophy, in which the movement is said to have its origin?" (xi.). "All who call themselves Christians should be constrained to admit the lawfulness of its foremost purpose, for the persistence of life beyond death was the spiritual lesson of Christ's resurrection" (p. 3). "It takes Christ's teaching as a whole; and if it be objected that the Church also does this, the reply is, 'The Church had also the doctrine of a vicarious atonement'" (p.12). "If for convenience we designate the high ranks (of the departed) Angels, and the lower as Evil Spirits, let us be careful not to lose sight of the fact that they differ only as elder and younger" (p. 76). "There is no room in the Universe for an essentially evil thing" (p. 77). "We must reject the conception of fallen creatures. By the Fall we understand the descent of spirit into matter" (p. 162). "The 'New Theology' is the old Wisdom to which Christ gave

Modern Spiritism Begins in 1847

Professor Richet and J. Arthur Hill, in the "Physical Phenomena of Spiritualism" (a well-known text-book), and many others actually date Modern Spiritism from 1847. It was in December of that year that mysterious rappings were first heard in a Methodist's house in New York State, in a quiet family of the name of Fox, which contained two young girls just arrived at maidenhood.

The mysterious rappings all over the house, which caused such crowds to assemble, lost much of their supposed spiritist power when it was discovered that these two girls could at will, without apparent movement, loudly crack their knee and toe joints; but it was never finally settled that this was the sole cause of the rappings. Recent researches by Sir Wm. Crookes, Sir Oliver Lodge and others have shown that certain individuals can produce distinct and loud raps in their joints at will, but the power is rare.

Old Spiritism

This caused a revival of old Spiritist practices that can be traced from ancient times. It was common amongst the Essenes, and Delitsch shows table-turning was practised in Jewish circles in the seventh century. Spiritism was known in Egypt in the fourth century. The successor to the Emperor Theodosius was announced by table-rapping. All over the Roman and Grecian Empires,

the sanction of His authority" (p. 183). "Spiritism is essentially Christian"; though, on page 151, André teaches re-incarnation!

I insert this note to show that Spiritism may be fairly described as regards its doctrine as "Theosophy and water."

in China, most pagan countries, amongst the Red Indians, and the sect of the Gnostics, Spiritism was found; and history records how universally it was practised in the Middle Ages, and the severe laws against it.

The French Revolution is said to have brought in an era of materialism that largely extinguished Spiritism in civilised countries. It was revived by Professors Mesmer and Swedenborg* in somewhat different forms with great power, and carried on later in France by its skilled exponent, Allan Kardec, a great apostle of reincarnation, which, although believed in by some 600 millions, is still without any proof.

Spiritism in England

It was little known in England until 1852, when it became popular in the familiar phenomenon of table-turning. It was the amusement of nearly every drawing-room. During the Crimean War it was a great resource in society circles. Simple, however, though this is in itself, and apparently little more than a parlour game, it leads on imperceptibly by further steps to manifestations so remarkable that it has often proved the beginning of an obsession that has led to the most disastrous physical and mental results. To their great credit, so far from denying or concealing this danger, the leaders of the cult are full of warnings of the risks attending practices that may begin with simple table-turning.

Modern Spiritism aroused very widespread interest

* Swedenborg was a great Spiritist, and was supposed to speak with the mighty dead in all ages.

when the Rev. W. Stainton Moses, B. A. Oxon.,
a member of the S.P.R.,* a man of undoubted integrity and the highest character, a college master at
University College, London, and a Mr. D. D. Home,
a nephew of the Earl of Home, also a man of high
character, joined the ranks of the new science as
mediums.

This is not the place for recounting their marvels;
but their advent and, at the same time, the wonderful
talents of the Rev. Henry Irving, the founder of the
Latter Day Saints, or so-called Holy Apostolic
Church, with all the wonders enacted in his services,
combined to interest all society, from the Throne
downwards, in this new cult.

Society for Psychical Research

Such a science, claiming such unheard-of powers,
demanded authoritative investigation; and Sir
Wm. Barrett, Mr. Ed. Gurney, and others joined, in
1891, in founding the Society for Psychical Research,
of which Mr. Arthur Balfour, Sir Wm. Crookes,
Professor Henry Sidgwick, and other most distinguished men have been presidents. Mr. Gladstone,
Bishop Boyd Carpenter, Professor Henri Bergson
were also active members. Its business was
closely to investigate all alleged phenomena of
the borderland, which it has continued to do
for nearly thirty years from its offices in Han-
over Square. So far as I am aware, however, it has
made no definite pronouncement upon Modern
Spiritism, for such is not its object; but it has
established as facts beyond question, the existence of

* Society for Psychical Research.

some unknown human powers, which will be considered later on; and also suggested others, not yet proved.

I have never been a member of the Psychical Research Society, but my solitary visit to it may be worth recording, for it was of great, though painful, interest to myself. The reader must bear with the digression. I had to go to their rooms to solve some question when I got an invitation to a dinner of the Society. I found I was placed next the treasurer of the S.P.R., a Mr. H P. Smith, whose face seemed familiar.

H. Pearsall-Smith

I must mention here that, several years before an American gentleman, with some very remarkable religious views, came over to England on business. I was present, with a barrister cousin of mine, at the first Bible-reading he held in this country in the Mayor's parlour in Manchester.

The subject was "The Walls of Jericho," and we were told, with great spiritual power, that, if we acted in simple faith on God's word, we should see the same wonders that Joshua saw.

This meeting changed for the better my cousin's whole course of life, and greatly affected my views. At Brighton and elsewhere Mr. Henry Pearsall-Smith's discourses profoundly influenced the religious world, and, notably, such men as the late Evan Hopkins, Prebendary Webb-Peploe, and some of our Bishops; and eventually led to the foundation of the now well-known Conventions (attended by thousands) at Keswick. Mr. Smith was, however, greatly overstrained later in life, and was at that time, so far as I knew, in an asylum.

The "H. P.," however, on the treasurer's card next to me at the dinner attracted my attention, and I ventured to ask Mr. Smith if he had ever heard of the well-known Henry Pearsall-Smith, who had moved in such a very different circle.

As Treasurer of the S.P.R.

"Why, yes," he said; "I am the man." He had evidently recovered, and taken the, for him, extraordinary position of an official in the S.P.R.

"But I was present," I said, greatly perplexed, "at your first meeting in Manchester when your spiritual power began to be felt."

"Yes," he said, "I remember it well; but have always been puzzled myself to know what the spiritual power really was."

"Well," I replied, "to my mind it seems that you inspired men to trust God as they had never trusted Him before."

"I suppose that was it," he answered, "though it was always a mystery to me; for I came over solely on business, but soon found myself at the head of a great religious movement."

"That is true," I said, "but you are now the treasurer of the S.P.R."

"That's all right," he rejoined; "but I should like to say a word of warning about Spiritism. My brother in America is a leading Spiritist, and he tells me that its study seems everywhere to lower the moral character, and to unhinge the mental balance in a very remarkable way."

The First Warnings

I believe Mr. Smith went so far as to say that his brother did not know one leading Spiritist in America who was not affected in some such way, more or less.

At any rate, it was from the lips of H. P.-Smith, now quite recovered, at this dinner of the S.P.R., that I received my first grave caution against Modern Spiritism. Maeterlinck points out that Spiritism has always been opposed by Science and Religion—by the former because its sphere is the physical; by the latter because it is forbidden. Augury or divination wearies the intellect, stunts enterprise, and distorts the conscience. As Isaiah says: "Thy spells and enchantments with which thou hast wearied thyself have led thee astray."

Mrs. Piper, in America, soon became the leading medium after Moses and Home in England; though, in October, 1891, she denied she had ever had any communications with the departed!

There is now a British National Association of Spirits (established 1873), and Mr. Stead carried on for a few years a Spiritist Bureau for Necromancy, or Intercourse with Departed Spirits, with terrible results to some. (See close of next chapter.)

Spirits are now numbered, *it is said*, by millions. In 1877 Hepworth Dixon declared that one-tenth in New England States were touched with Spiritism. In 1900, in the States, twenty-five working Spiritist societies existed, over 10,000 mediums were at work, and eighty-two wealthy churches, with Sunday Schools, were flourishing. Spiritist schools were common, and Spiritist ordinations of ministers recognised.

Sir Oliver J. Lodge

During the war, as a well-known scientific writer points out, there was a felt need in Modern Spiritist circles of some commanding authority, some Luke or Paul, to appear in England to support the cult. He must be a scientist to suit the temper of the time. Sir Wm. Crookes was over eighty, and Sir Wm. Barrett not an active or popular teacher.

The want was supplied by the sudden arrival in the front rank of Spiritists of Sir Oliver Lodge. The remarkable details from America of his opportune conversion afford food for thought.

It is pointed out by some that Spiritism is to-day in the stage that storms, electricity, and epidemics were only a century ago. We know their laws now, and no longer ascribe their phenomena immediately to any supernatural agency.

Already many of the phenomena of Spiritism have been satisfactorily discounted by science; and it seems not improbable that in another hundred years there may be few left that are still deemed supernatural.

Not only so, but, as Professor Richet well points out, it is a more difficult task in the present state of our knowledge to form a sane estimate of Modern Spiritism than to learn Arabic. Few of my readers have done the latter, and none should suppose that this book alone will enable them to do the former.

The Latest Book on Spiritism

I will bring these few notes up to date by touching on the latest book on Spiritism by a journalist, a Mr. Sydney Moseley, whom Sir A. Conan Doyle, in a preface to his book, vouches for as "a very sane observer, whose conclusions deserve the most earnest attention."

My Friend Davies

This "very sane observer" begins by describing life after death as a new doctrine, apparently discovered by Spiritism, totally ignoring that it has been a foundation truth of Christianity for well-nigh 2,000 years, and is only unknown to unbelievers. Later he distinctly hears rapping on the window of his railway carriage, and believes it to be "spirits," until his friend and adviser, a Mr. Davies, points out it is a man knocking his pipe in the next compartment! He hears an Indian chief talking in negro dialect, and several other wonders. I should not record these puerilities did not Sir A. Conan Doyle tell us they proceed from "a very sane observer."

His friend Davies at first would have nothing to do with Spiritism, for he found it was condemned by the Bible (a rare but very good reason), until he was shown St. Luke xxiv. 25: "O fools and slow of heart to believe all that the prophets have spoken." Will it be credited that he interpreted this to mean that they were fools *because* they believed the Old Testament prophets, instead of (as our Lord said) being fools *not to believe* them—a meaning the context plainly shows. This absurdity is gravely quoted by our "very sane observer" with evident approval.

I do not say that Mr. Sydney Moseley is a worthy representative of Spiritism; and I fear the book shows that Sir A. Conan Doyle, though a distinguished novelist, is not a very safe judge of character.

Like many other "cults," Spiritism suffers from its friends.

American Origin

What impresses me in going through the accumulated mass of literature on the subject is the everlasting recurrence of the same dozen names of leading Spiritists and mediums, who seem to constitute all the authorities on Modern Spiritism. In common with other new religions, its rise seems to be, in modern times, from the States, where it flourishes much better than in the more frigid and exhausted soil of Europe.

It now remains for me to chronicle a few of the best-authenticated and most remarkable phenomena in Modern Spiritism and some other allied conditions, and attempt some explanation of these so far as is possible in the present state of our knowledge. Those who look for final and absolute pronouncements must remember that the whole subject is so new and strange to most of us that such are neither yet possible nor desirable. We shall consider Spiritism first of all rather on its physical side as a Science; and then we shall take up the subject on its psychical and moral side as a Religion: and here it may be both possible and desirable to come to a reasonable judgment.

CHAPTER III

THE PHENOMENA OF MODERN SPIRITISM

A Modern Séance

THOSE who have not attended a séance of
Spiritists, with a good medium, can have but a faint
concept of its extraordinary character. The remarkable combination of the serious with the comic, the
religious with the profane or worse, the mysterious
with the commonplace, the true with the false;
together with the darkened room, the unexpected and
certainly weird appearances, sounds, lights, and often
smells, the tight holding of hands for hours (no
gloves), the strained attention, the earnest expectation of one knows not what, must all be experienced
to be realised. To crown the performance is the
prayer, which always, to me, borders on the blasphemous, followed by the appalling attempts at
singing American revival hymns by aged scientists
and others, which do more than border on the
ludicrous.

Séances indeed, between 1860 and 1870, were
mostly of the nature of revival meetings: partly
religious, partly emotional, and very sensational.
When T. A. Trollope, the novelist, was at a séance

with D. D. Home we are told that "tears of holy joy coursed down his manly cheeks."

The prayer is, of course, defended as necessary, because it is supposed to keep out evil spirits. It may be offered by the medium, or rather by some spirit supposed to be controlling (*i.e.*, using) her at the time. There is almost sure to be, during a prolonged séance, all sorts of meaningless freaks, toys, flowers, etc., flying in the air, and musical instruments heard about the room.

Spirit-Controls

Professor Jacks, while he was President of the Society for Psychical Research, attended three séances with a special medium. He had first to dismiss any hypothesis of fraud, which is so common amongst professional mediums; but this was not enough. If he wished to see true phenomena he found he must assume the reality of the spirit-control of the medium before he could get any communications, which was very unsatisfactory to him, for the control professed to be the spirit of some departed person. Having accepted this, one had to take the truth of the whole of what followed for granted! The "controls" are generally remote people, such as a French doctor of 200 years ago, an Oriental girl, a North American Indian, or a priest of the Pharaohs. On the other hand, the "spirit" is some one known to the audience. Dr. Jacks found the "stage patter" and the phraseology of disguised theosophy (on which Modern Spiritism is largely based) very annoying. He could not get into communication with any of his relations; but suddenly the "spirit" of the last person in the world he expected spoke by the "control" (through the medium) in a strong man's voice.

Physical and Psychic Phenomena

All phenomena at séances may be broadly classed as two—physical and psychical. The former includes all movements, sounds and materialisations; the latter, spirit-writing and all communications "from the dead" by rappings, etc.

However frivolous and silly most séances may be, it is worth noting that, when held for a definite purpose, to prove some point in Modern Spiritism, and with adepts, all this disappears, and they become perfectly orderly and serious. There appears to be a method in the madness.

Perhaps the most extraordinary part is the obsession of the audience, of which I shall say more in another chapter. Although all witness the same phenomena, their accounts of these are as various and contradictory as if they had been at different séances.

It will be understood throughout that "phenomenal" is practically equivalent to "miraculous."

Mediums

The next points to consider are the mediums— male or female; generally the latter. These I believe to be people naturally, or by practice, capable of *throwing themselves* into what is called a trance, that is, a state of more or less complete unconsciousness, similar to that formerly induced in ordinary hypnosis, which is effected by another.

This is by no means an easy process. The Rev.
W. Wynn says of a medium that it took him
nearly ten minutes to pass under control (or, as I
believe, into a hypnotic condition), "after many
strange bodily contortions which are not pleasant
to witness, but are quite natural *if* we are to assume
that a discarnate spirit controls his body." Mediums
are, therefore, practised in the art of auto-hypnosis,
the effect of which appears to be to throw the conscious mind into abeyance, and to bring into activity
the unconscious mind (see Chapter I.), called by
Myers "subliminal," by others "sub-conscious."
Now it is an established fact that in the state of
hypnosis a person so conditioned can remember
things entirely forgotten by his consciousness, can
unconsciously read the minds (conscious or unconscious) of others by telepathy, and can do many
apparent marvels, the source of which he himself, in this state, is unconscious of. It is obvious, to go no further, how much a séance depends
on the medium's power to throw herself absolutely
into this condition, in which she can speak with certainty of things quite unknown to herself, and thus
apparently act as a "medium" between the audience
and some extra-human intelligence. In this case,
of course, the real solution is the state in which the
"medium" is, which enables all the marvellous
information to come unconsciously through her by
telepathy* and allied processes, from the minds

---

* Telepathy, or thought-transference, at a distance and without words has become a scientific fact through the arduous
labours of the Psychical Research Society, known generally
as the S.P.R.

(conscious or unconscious) of the inquirers. This explanation, which may appear to some to be complicated and far-fetched, is really simple and direct, and is based on established facts. But though it accounts for most of the psychical phenomena that are not fraudulent, it does not apparently, as we shall see, account for all. It certainly shows, however, that the term "medium" is objectionable since the discovery of telepathy; for the person acting is not generally a "medium" between another intelligence and our own; seeing that all generally comes, through the power of hypnosis and telepathy, from herself and her audience. To call her* a "medium" begs the whole question.

The Question of Fraud

These beings of such exceptional powers mostly spend their lives in this abnormal condition at a great expense of vitality, for the state of trance is most exhausting and unnatural. Moreover, it is uncertain, and cannot be always induced. It is obvious, therefore, that where money depends on the séance, and when fraud is so much more certain to produce results and easy to practice, why it is so often resorted to. Indeed, in America and even here, fraud is so general that many, who otherwise would investigate the phenomena, recoil in disgust from the whole subject, and declare Spiritism to be nothing but fraud, which is not true.† The

* I say "her" throughout instead of "him," owing to the preponderance of women mediums.

† It is only fair, in this connection, to distinguish between professional mediums, who work for money, and to whom these remarks specially apply, and private mediums, who do not take money or give public séances, but who still may, at times, deceive.

French Spiritist writer, C. Flammarion, greatly regrets "that we cannot trust the loyalty of mediums. They nearly all cheat." While Mrs. Sidgwick says: "The chief scandal of Spiritism is the encouragement it gives to the immoral trade of mediumship."

The powers of a medium are occasionally lifelong, but generally, curious to say, only for a term. The Rev. Stainton Moses had marvellous power from thirty-three to forty-four, when it suddenly departed, though he lived for nine years afterwards.

Notable Mediums

Eusapia Palladino, the Italian medium, gradually lost her powers; while those of Mrs. Piper, the American medium, were suddenly wrecked.

It may be said here that the belief that psychical communications, *other than those of telepathic origin*, already described are possible, mainly rests on the work of one medium, Mrs. Piper, and that belief in physical manifestations (levitation, sounds, lights, etc.) being real, and not fraudulent, rests on the work of Eusapia Palladino, of Naples. Both of these, however, as pointed out by Mr. Frank Podmore ("The Newer Spiritism," p. 33), have been exposed in fraudulent practices.*

Spiritist Phenomena

We now turn to Spiritist phenomena; and here, it is obvious, I must be very brief, and do little more

* On the other hand, the bulk of their work under rigid test conditions has been proved, on undoubted scientific authority, to be genuine.

than outline some of the leading wonders, as the subject is so vast. I will speak first of those phenomena we may term physical, nearly always, be it remembered, induced by the presence of a recognised medium (not necessarily, however, in a trance) in the room. There are rare instances where no known medium has been present. I say "known" medium, because it has afterwards been found that a person possessing such powers, which were at the time unknown to herself, was in the room.

Every sort of furniture has moved with and without contact, and even against efforts to prevent it, apparently by some inherent power. In fact inanimate objects seem for the time to be endowed with some sort of intelligence and purpose.

These absolutely independent movements of furniture are vouched for as established facts by Sir Wm. Crookes, one of the world's first scientists, and a man of keen observation, cautious disposition, and absolutely reliable accuracy.

A table or chair begins to move towards the skilled observer, who pushes it back five or six times, when it slowly returns each time. This is in daylight, and there is no string or cord attached.

Floating Furniture

Sir Wm. Barrett reports a case that convinced him of some unknown force. Loud raps (like electric discharges) came from a table, four feet square, when no one touched it. Then, in obedience to orders, it first lifted its two front legs, then its two back ones, ten inches off the ground, and then it floated across the room. This was in Sir Wm. Barrett's own house in Dublin. Then the table rapped out messages, which, however, were valueless and mere platitudes. Miss L., in whose presence (as the medium) these wonders occurred, one may mention, is a Methodist.

Sir William conducted further experiments with Dr. Crawford (Lecturer in Mechanical Engineering at Belfast College), and the latter found that, as the table rose in the air, and decreased in weight, so the medium increased by many pounds.* At one séance the table struck the floor suddenly a tremendous bang, then rose eighteen inches and remained level in the air. Dr. Crawford tried to push it down, but could not do so. He then climbed up and sat on the table as it floated. All this was in his own house, with his own family, and no money was paid to any one.

The Spirit in the Wood

Dr. Marcel Violett says the raps are heard *in* the table itself. He says an interior movement takes place in the wood of the table, and he has had a table, fractured by this force, repaired more than once. Words and phrases were rapped out (on an alphabetical system) which were of no literary, scientific, or philosophic value.

Sometimes, he says, if we think we know the word that is being spelt, and write it down to save time, the table objects, and becomes agitated (shakes) all over. (Just as a stammerer does when we suggest

* In materialisation, on the other hand, Sir Wm. Crookes has found her decrease as much as 23 lbs.

to him what he is trying to say.) These séances were mostly conducted in darkness.

Professor Maeterlinck, one summer, in an old abbey, was entertaining some guests, who were making a small table spin on its feet by placing their hands on it. He was smoking in another part of the room. Suddenly the table rapped out that it held the spirit of a monk who was buried in the east gallery of the cloisters in 1693. The whole party then got up and went there, and discovered a very old tombstone inscribed A.D. 1693. Maeterlinck adds: "My guests only arrived that night on their first visit to the abbey, and had seen nothing, and I believed myself wholly ignorant of the tombstone."*

Regarding levitation, Professor Flammarion, of Paris, says: "The phenomenon of levitation is, to me, absolutely proved, though it cannot be explained." In 1906, at the Psychological Institute, in Paris, a heavy table was lifted twenty inches from the ground by two people placing their hands upon it.

Professor Lombroso also testifies to furniture floating. But there are greater marvels yet.

Floating Men

Sir Wm. Crookes has seen Mr. Douglas D. Home, a well-known medium, and supposed nephew of the Earl of Home, sitting in the air with nothing under him.

In December, 1868, at 5, Buckingham Gate, in the

---

* Observe Maeterlinck was *not sure;* the medium present could have given the information from the professor's unconscious mind by telepathy if the latter had ever heard of the monk.

presence of Lord Crawford, the Earl of Dunraven, and Captain Wynn, D. D. Home was seen floating round the room near the ceiling, carrying an arm-chair with him.

On December 16th the same people saw Home float out of the window, eighty-five feet above the ground, and travel $7\frac{1}{2}$ feet to the next window, and there glide in feet foremost, and then sit down. *This is perhaps the greatest physical marvel known in Spiritism.* For the suggested explanation of this, and all other wonders, I must ask my readers to wait in patience till they reach Chapter V.

Materialisation

Materialisation seems to me, if possible, a still greater wonder, inasmuch as it apparently involves the production, from some unknown source, of a living being.

(I may say at once that most of these move-ments and physical appearances are delusions or frauds, as I shall show presently.)

Talking to Mr. Robert King, the well-known occultist, the other day, he told me that there were some six mediums in these isles who had the power to materialise spirits; that all were drunkards, and would deceive you by fraud if they could.

The three cases on which apparently genuine materialisation really rests are Sir Wm. Crookes' "Katie King," Professor Richet's "Arab" and Dr. Morselli's mother—Eusapia being the medium here. Eusapia is a Neapolitan peasant woman, publicly convicted of fraud on several occasions.

"Katie King"

With Sir Wm. Crookes, Miss Cook was the medium, and for three years she materialised, in Sir Wm. Crookes' house, at intervals a being, "Katie King," whom Crookes closely examined. She spoke to him and his scientific guests, and walked about with them; then suddenly disappeared. Crookes, with six or seven other eminent scientists, saw "Katie King" and the medium side by side, and then, under three gas-jets, watched "Katie King" slowly disappear. She was photographed, and Crookes counted her heart, which beat at seventy-five, when the medium's was ninety. She had ordinary flesh and bones, and he was convinced that her body (at any rate) was not the medium's.* When she finally left she went with Sir William to the cabinet, and bent over the medium and said: "Wake up, Florrie, I must leave you now." Miss Cook then woke up, and begged her to stay a little longer. "No, dear, I can't. My work is done. God bless you." Crookes then helped Miss Cook to rise, and, when he turned, "Katie King" was gone. Other materialisations seem more or less open to doubt. I must point out here that no amount of materialisation, or of movement, or levitation, however wonderful, true, and inexplicable, constitute, either separately or collectively, *any evidence whatever of a spirit world or of life after death*. Any evidence of this is wholly psychical, and comes by raps which spell the words, or by writing, more or less automatic. Both of these means are very easily fraudulently produced; but there seems

* He seems in some doubt about the spirit.

to be sufficient evidence that in many cases they are genuine productions by some unknown superhuman power.

Other Physical Phenomena

There are various other physical phenomena of rare occurrence. Genuine spirit photographs seem possible, though it is almost impossible to prove they are such, as they are so easily imitated. Col. de Roches, in 1894, and Dr. Barlemont obtained the simultaneous photo of the body of a medium and of her separated "astral body."

The Rev. W. Stainton Moses (already quoted), an Oxford M.A. of the highest character and a most credible witness, says at another séance: "Scent kept oozing out of the medium's head. The more it was wiped away, the more it poured forth. Musical sounds were also heard all around."

A lengthening of the body is occasionally seen; D. D. Home elongated himself eleven inches! He also played before Sir Wm. Crookes on a harmonium some distance away, which was enclosed and locked in a metal case.

Crookes at another time put his finger on *The Times*, and said, "Write the word under my finger." Home immediately wrote "however," which *was* the word, which Crookes did *not* know, thus excluding telepathy.

Crookes has seen, in his own dining-room, an accordion playing while held firmly in his own hands. Also a pendulum move in a glass case.

The knotting of a rope with fixed and sealed ends in full daylight was performed, in December, 1877, in the presence of Professors Zöllner, Weber, Fechner and Schreibner, by a well-known medium; nor is this case unique.*

Conan Doyle at Glasgow

The other day, in an upper room in Glasgow, Sir A. Conan Doyle and fifteen others heard the sound of a rushing wind, and they all saw tongues of fire descend on each other's heads. This is seriously recorded for our instruction!

I will not spend time on all the silly and freakish scenes at séances, where the mediums or the spirits seem to try to fool the audience in every way, but may just record that a well-known doctor found one day the bedroom where his three sons slept turned upside down. Four people watched the mattress being pulled off the bed by invisible hands, and the chairs being turned upside down.

Then his father suddenly appeared to his housemaid in a blaze of glorious light. The maid afterwards turned out to be a medium, and many séances were held.

All attempts to prove fraud or trickery entirely failed. He proceeds to say, "I and Jane" (the housemaid) "resolved to have nothing more to do with spirits, but the knocks kept coming, so we held one more séance, Jane, my wife, and I. Jane became unconscious, and some spirit began talking, through her, about some intricate business I was interested in, in German-English, and said he had been trying to speak to me for thirteen years. Our

---

* This and other performances are more like conjuring tricks than Spiritist phenomena.

séances seemed crowded with spirits in a dense throng all round the medium, and made all kinds of interruptions." The doctor was an evangelical Christian man, and an enemy to Spiritism.

Do not Throw the Book away

If the reader has got thus far, I beg of him not to throw away the book at this juncture and declare he will not read another word of such stuff, for, unless he is prepared to wade through much of a similar character, he can never know much about Spiritism. I can assure him the "stuff" has been carefully selected from hundreds of the best cases in Spiritism, and consists solely of well-authenticated facts, certified to by witnesses as credible and worthy of belief as the reader himself; and here may I beg him not to deny the truth of what he cannot understand; for, after all, the human intellect does not comprehend all things. Moreover, will he bear in mind that, in endeavouring to give a fair presentment of Modern Spiritism, it is absolutely essential the reader should know its real powers, however contrary such may appear to be to his reason? Has he grasped the fact that Sir Wm. Crookes, with another distinguished scientist, went into the subject absolutely determined to unmask the "rubbishing imposture"; and both became firm believers in the facts I have detailed, although, I am thankful to say, not in the religion or dogmas of Spiritism, to which I shall allude later on.

More Marvels

If the reader is reassured, and his patience will stand a little more, I will proceed. Professor

Alexander had two little girls with some of the powers of mediums. They saw a spirit form, which was also seen by a dog, who barked at it, and by a baby, who cried out, "Man, man!" and pointed at it.

In General Boldero's house at Cupar, with D. D. Home in the room, a bright light was seen, the table moved off to the piano, on which notes were struck, and two voices were heard talking, though Home kept speaking all the time to show it was not his voice. Mrs. Boldero walked over to the piano, and saw the notes depressed and heard lovely chords. The harp was played next, the strings vibrating.

A well-known scientist seriously thinks it a proof of an "astral body" when he says he saw his wife and children in a cab while he was senseless in a dentist's chair. My reader may make fun of this to his heart's content, for I agree with him that such a vision is a common result of laughing gas and other anæsthetics.

Psychic Phenomena

I now turn from physical phenomena to those of a psychical nature, with which are connected all raps by which words are laboriously spelt out, as well as with automatic writing. All such, more or less, relate to supposed communications from the dead, or necromancy. To understand what follows the reader must grasp that all messages have to pass through four personalities. First of all, the supposed spirit of the departed "speaks" to the "control" of the medium—sometimes, as in Mrs. Piper's case,

a North American Indian (also dead), who speaks in
negro language for some unknown reason! The
control then communicates this message to the
medium, who then makes it known to the sitter, who
then tells his friends, of whom the reader may be
one. Sometimes the "control," using the medium's
hand to write, or rapping the table himself, shortens
the process; as a rule, however, the message passes,
with more or less distortion, through four minds—
the spirit's, the control's, the medium's, and the
inquirer's.

Hodgson and Moses

Later on I shall fully discuss the *pros* and *cons*
of the truth of alleged communications from the
dead; here I shall only give, very shortly, some
carefully selected facts connected with this and other
subjects.

Professor Hodgson, of Boston, is said to have
begun to speak through the medium Mrs. Piper, who
had acted solely under his guidance for twenty years,
eight days after his death, and to have continued
since.

At a sitting in August, 1874, of Mr. Stainton Moses
with an Isle of Wight doctor, they received a communication from Abraham Florentin, who stated
he had fought in 1812, and died at Brooklyn, New
York, on August 5th, 1874. No one had ever heard
of him; but advertisements inserted in American
papers brought to light that a man of this name had
been in the American Forces, and the headquarters
of the U. S. Army said that a Private Abraham
Florentin had served in the American War. His

widow was found, and stated he had died on August 5th, 1874. Full reports of this case are in the *Proceedings of the Psychical Research Society*, Vol. XI.

With regard to the story of Abraham Florentin, F. W. H. Myers remarks: "I hold that the surviving spirit of A. F. really did speak through Mr. Stainton Moses." By now Mr. Myers probably knows if this belief is true.

Other Cases

When E. R. Bates was taking a message the table rapped out "H A." Bates said "The next letter is 'V,'" but a most emphatic "no" came; so they went on through the alphabet, and got to Y without response; but at Z a clear "yes" came. Then "A" came, and the message read, "You hazard my respect if you don't give up occult science."

A spirit message given through a private medium in England was finished, three days later, by Mrs. Piper, in Boston with the remark from the spirit, "I am afraid I did not make myself quite clear three days ago."

A well-known medium had living friends who could write messages by his hand easier than he could write himself, and did so.

It must be remembered that automatic writing is always preferred to raps, being so much quicker.

Of course, its chief objective has always been, for the last fifty years, the hope that it may bring the living into touch with some one beyond the grave.

Sir Hugh Lane

Mrs. Travers-Smith, on the evening of the sinking of the *Lusitania*, had a message at a séance: "Pray for the soul of Sir Hugh Lane;" and in answer to the question, "Who is speaking?" came "I am Sir Hugh Lane." She did not know he was a passenger. She then got a further message from him, and he said he was drowned, and didn't suffer. News of his death came days after.

Professor Jacks, then President of the S.P.R., says a spirit told him about a MS. lying in his study drawer, of which no one knew but himself, and quoted from it.

"Spirits," says Professor Jacks, "are apt to get mixed. For instance, if speaking to Sir Walter Scott, the spirit would declare he died one thousand miles from Abbotsford; and, when asked which Scott he was, would reply, 'Sir Gilbert.'"

Professor Jacks said he did not know what to make of all this. It seemed to him, after all these years, they were only beginning; and the haste some people were showing to prove that "survival after death" was the only explanation was only damaging inquiry.

After all, it is not perhaps what is said on these occasions that is of so much importance, as the mere fact that anything is said at all.

When I was at Elizabeth College, in Guernsey, the niece of our then ambassador at Berlin, a lady well known at the Prussian Court in 1850, used to show me sheets and sheets of automatic writing, and beautifully drawn and painted fruit and flowers, done with great rapidity by her hand, used involuntarily. When, however, raps and voices succeeded she got frightened and gave it all up. An Arab gentleman, known to me, did *not* give it up, with the result he became possessed with an evil spirit, of which case I will say more in Chapter VII.

"Raymond"

I proceed now to what follows not without pain; for I have known Sir Oliver Lodge, and spoken at his charming house at Birmingham; and I can fully understand the irresistible appeal once more to speak to his son that prompted all recorded in "Raymond." Many widows have come to me respecting communications with their sons who died in the Great War, asking if the messages they received were indeed from the dead, and whether it was right for them, as Christian women, to hold such communications. Tenderly, very tenderly, must such cases be dealt with, and I hold that "Raymond" calls for similar treatment.

To the bereaved mothers I could only lay stress on all there was of hope and comfort, while gently suggesting that what they heard was probably but the reflex of the image their boy had himself stamped upon their hearts, and, therefore, subjective and not objective.* Perhaps I may be allowed to add how deeply I appreciate the lofty, if mistaken, motives that led Sir Oliver to risk his professional fame by the publication of such a book.

Examination of Testimony

I do *not* say, with regard to "Raymond," that the recorded communications were all subjective pro-

* So far all such cases have been most easily explained by the action of the unconscious mind; but I am grieved to add that, even in these sad cases, the practice is not without danger. A friend of mine, a gallant cavalry officer, lost his reason at Mr.

ducts of the unconscious minds of those interested; for, coming from an eminent scientist, and under careful test conditions, the record stands so far in a different category; but, since his private sorrow has been brought by Sir Oliver Lodge himself so prominently before the public, I feel that one may, without offence, carefully examine some of the testimony supposed to proceed from the boy Raymond.

I must remind my reader that all communications recorded come through the four-fold channel I have already described, and that the controls in this case were principally "Feda" and "Moonstone." We first notice that "Feda," the principal control, is a little Oriental girl, who is said to have died in childhood, and yet is perfectly familiar with the English language, thought, and slang.

"Moonstone" is an Indian Yogi, who died at over 100, and who is also proficient in English. Both of these, curiously enough, seemed to be at call and on duty at any hour, day or night, in any place. In addition there is a Redfeather who talks in negro dialect, though presumably a North-American Indian.

Disappointing and Contradictory

Raymond, the brilliant, earnest, energetic young engineer, does not after death make a single communication of serious import or utility. He, the loving son, does not even volunteer his services (on the other side). He is able to visit Germany and inspect the lines; but he brings back no information,

Stead's Spirit Bureau from continually hearing what he thought was his mother's voice.

and seems idle and callously indifferent, both nationally and domestically. He appears to be still in uniform, being known as an officer, though his uniform was burned in Flanders. Later on he has "white robes."

Indeed, Raymond's story of the six or seven revolving spheres around the globe (purely theo-sphical) struck Sir Oliver Lodge as "nonsense," for these gigantic revolving spheres would necessarily shut out the sun, as well as alter all astronomical conditions.

Raymond's reports of the next world reveal it as practically all English, with a few Indians and French.

Some Absurdities

Raymond, referring to his family, shows an "H" instead of saying "his sister Honor," which he could just as well do, if the message came from him.*

When he speaks of "something rising, which, *when it comes* to the ether, etc.," Sir Oliver must have had a queer feeling of disgust, his doctrine (which is generally accepted) being that the ether is "*all-pervading*."

When asked about table-tilting, etc., the trained engineer can only repeat the stock chestnut that "it gathers magnetism, and we [spirits] move it."

He never mentions any great departed spirits, such as Lord Kelvin, Faraday, Tyndall, and hosts of others.

The dead (though dead thirty years) are always

* One can appreciate the wise caution shown, if, however, the message came solely from the medium.

described, not as they are, but as they exist in the
sitters' minds when they were known to them on
earth.

Evil Spirits

But enough for the present; we must conclude
this most indigestible chapter with one word about
the spirits.

The doctrine of Modern Spiritism is that the only
spirits "on the other side" are those of the departed!

"Devils," says Thomas Jay Hudson, a leading
American scientist, "are out of fashion, and their
place is taken by bad spirits of dead men."

In Spiritism, as Allan Kardec, the great French
apostle, clearly teaches, there are no devils. The
bad spirits are only imperfectly developed "angels,"
which are the spirits of the good.

"Some spirits," wrote Stainton Moses, "will say
anything without any moral conscience. Such
motiveless lying bespeaks a deeply evil nature.
Such an imposter, acting with an air of sincerity,
must be as Satan clothed in light."

Dr. Peebles, a veteran Spiritist, recently says that
"an evilly inclined spirit may often be present.
Many Spiritist séances are the seed-grounds of
demons; their manifestations are from the hells.
They constitute the very essence of witchcraft under
a more polished name" ("The Demonism of the
Ages," p. 217).

Possession

It is clear the whole atmosphere of the séance, and
the ultimate object of Spiritism, is the reduction to
passivity and the eventual entire surrender of the

will, thus gaining its control with a view to spirit-possession.

As Chapter VII. is largely devoted to this subject, I say no more about the condition, which students of the subject and many of our leading alienists know well, and which is as clearly marked and undeniable to-day as are the cases recorded in the Gospels. It is difficult to believe that, when their awful character is known, Spiritists can possibly believe such beings are the spirits of the dead—it is a degradation of, and an insult to, humanity!

I have made no comments on the facts (and fancies) I have recorded, for this is not the place; and I fear that I have greatly failed to describe sufficiently the commonplace and trivial character of most séances.

Unhealthy Atmosphere

The whole atmosphere to me seems profoundly unhealthy, and, to a certain extent, repellent to common sense and repugnant to reason, on account of the inane frivolities that beset ordinary séances. Similar, indeed, are the impenetrable wonders of a conjurer, but with a great difference.

A conjurer does things that baffle our reasoning powers and defy our senses to explain; but does it all by sleight of hand and apparatus, and by means well understood by us. In a séance it is not so. We there see marvels as inexplicable to us as conjuring tricks; but here there is no conjurer apparent; on the contrary, a medium is seen lying or sitting in a trance, more or less asleep, while weird physical phenomena go on all around, seeking from us a belief that they proceed from superhuman powers of which we know nothing.

I have pointed out that, broadly, all phenomena may ultimately be ranged under the two heads of the physical and the psychical; but I have not shown that the entrance to these two is also two-fold, and is nearly always either by table-turning, or planchette writing, or by other similar apparatus.

Hidden Dangers of Spiritism

Hundreds of innocent young people regard these as popular, quite harmless, and often very amusing drawing-room diversions, being ignorant that in very many cases they have proved to be the portals to a growing and most undesirable acquaintance with another world. Most of those who indulge in these simple beginnings have not the slightest intention of proceeding further, and of ever becoming Spiritists, still less of dabbling in the mysteries of the other world; nor have they any wish to transgress in any way, or to act contrary to, their own moral or religious principles. But the *"descensus averni"* is unusually *"facilis"* in this case, and, before they have any idea of it, many find themselves more and more interested and involved in phenomena of increasing significance. Raps are continually heard, often at night. They begin to experience a haunted feeling; and yet, though repelled, they are still more strongly attracted by a growing love for a pursuit which they are beginning to feel is unlawful, and certainly is very mysterious; and one which for many reasons they often find it advisable to keep secret.

It is not long before the whole current of the life becomes a little changed, and the character alters for the worse.

The Wreck of the Ill-balanced

In sound, well-balanced characters matters may not proceed further. Indeed, at such a stage, as with a clever friend of mine, the network may be broken and the victim freed.

But, alas! in weak and ill-balanced natures, easily influenced, the spell has often become too strong; and the simple table-turning or planchette writing has in these much to answer for in a wrecked life.

This picture is not overdrawn, and not so uncommon as the ignorant may suppose. The Great War has, alas! from causes we can only regard with reverence and sympathy, brought many into the toils of Spiritism. Let me again say that it is very difficult to refuse any source of comfort to a distressed heart, and so easy to believe that the subjective is indeed objective, and that the loving messages received, and perhaps visions which are seen, are proofs of the presence of the loved and mourned one "on the other side," that it seems the height of cruelty to interpose with one's scientific knowledge and wise counsels. And yet I have had to do it, in all gentleness, and with firm decision point out the real source of the phenomena in the unconscious mind and its newly-discovered powers, and the significant fact that it must be for some very wise and necessary reason that communication with the dead is so strongly forbidden in the Old Testament,

and nowhere countenanced in the New.   I need not
say more here, as Chapter X. is on the "Dangers of
Spiritism;" but, as some of my readers may not
get so far, I thought it well to interpose a much-
needed word of caution here.

CHAPTER IV

THE SPIRITISTS' OTHER WORLD

The World After Death

"When you establish a world after death, you alter the proportion of everything," remarks a well-known scientist. Few will dispute the statement, but many will rub their eyes and wonder if they've been asleep, for they thought that this fact had been established ages ago, and was a belief practically common to every religion from time immemorial.

"That may be so," I suppose a scientist might reply; "but until established scientifically it does not exist for us."

Scientific Evidence

There is, of course, a wide range of subjects which are not yet "established" by the general consensus of scientists, but which "exist," though not for them. We might even include among these the separate life of the "spirit." This, of course, is denied entirely by all "monists" (represented by Hæckel and others), who regard thought as a secretion of the brain, somewhat comparable to bile from the liver. It is also doubted by some others, though monism is now a little out of date.

But even if not established on general scientific authority, the fact of another world is asserted, as is pointed out in the Gospels, by Moses and the prophets, and by Christ Himself, who replies, when asked to give a scientific demonstration of it, that such would be useless; for if people would not believe adequate testimony, a miracle would not convince them (St. Luke xvi.). But there is more in this question of so-called "scientific evidence" than this.

We All Live By Faith

We, the public, are all, surprising to say, men of "faith," rather than of "evidence." None of us, speaking broadly, *know* that water is composed of two parts of a gas called hydrogen and one part of a gas called oxygen by any other means than faith; we have not arrived at it by experiment. Or take some rather rarer scientific fact, say the moons of Jupiter. To all but some half-dozen these moons round that great planet are matters of faith. I am not, however, aware that the existence of such moons is a matter of doubt to any one, so great is the faith of the public in the word of those few astronomers who alone have seen them. I maintain, then, that we live by faith in the recorded evidence of others, and not by evidence.

I think we may not have noticed this fact before, and how the whole life of every atheist, of every sceptic, equally with that of all other people, is essentially a life of faith of the most implicit kind. Faith is indeed such an essential in all commercial and ordinary life that it is not noticed. No one thinks it wonderful that we hand over twenty good silver shillings without a doubt in exchange for a dirty, greasy scrap of paper that an abstraction, called the Government, asserts is a one-pound note. No one thinks it wonderful that a merchant will send away £1,000 worth of goods on his faith in the signature on a bit of paper of a man he has never seen, but whose writing he believes it to be. Life is all faith from beginning to end, and without it this nation could not go on for a single day.

We Believe Any One but Christ

It almost looks as if we could believe with the utmost ease in the word of anybody save the One whom we profess to exalt with the utmost honour as the King of men—the man Christ Jesus. I have never heard any one say a word against Him; but I have known so many who could not trust His word. His solemn statement respecting the next world, and the details He gives us concerning it, are treated as so entirely unworthy of credit that, as I pointed out in the second chapter, a very recent writer, specially commended to us by Sir A. Conan Doyle, writes of the other world as if its existence were now being discovered by Spiritists for the first time, without making the slightest allusion to the fact that 2,000 years ago Christ told us a great deal about it, and that almost every fact He told us contradicts the supposed discoveries of Modern Spiritism. It is difficult to understand such an attitude of mind anywhere, but in a Christian country religion must be at a very low ebb, to say nothing more, when His Word, who calls Himself "the Truth," is not even worth the trouble of doubting, but is simply ignored, as if He had never spoken and no Gospel had ever been written.*

Spiritism the Result of Unbelief

After labouring in vain to prove the evangelists false, critics have been obliged to accept them as genuine, and the Lord Jesus Christ as a historical personage, whom apparently all still delight to honour, more or less, with their lips, but whose Word is absolutely valueless compared with that of mediums, or even ordinary men of business! I may go further, and say it is only because men do not believe the Word of God that Spiritism has obtained any footing. It is absurd to speak of "priestcraft" as the cause, for Spiritism has most following in America, where there is practically none.

It is not my intention here in this chapter to describe the other world as Christ showed it to us. On the contrary, we have very briefly to find out what Spiritists believe it to be.

Spiritist Glimpses

We are indeed told with great confidence that "in a few years people on earth will know through Spiritism much more about the spirit world than

* This seems exactly on a par with the following from the *Times* of April 19th, 1919: "To-day there is better thinking and writing on social or national subjects than ever was in the world before.... But the eye is not on the History of the whole soul.... To read it you would not guess you were in a Christian country, with a long Christian tradition shaping its society. You would receive the impression that its religion had no more to do with its affairs than a harem, that is kept behind the purdah.... Hardly a reference is made to the Kingdom of God."

they do now." We will see first what they have already been taught.

Maeterlinck, in his "Unknown Guest," says: "The glimpses Spiritism gives us of the next world are none too assuring. The dead there, to-day, seem strangely like those Ulysses conjured up out of the Cimmerian darkness; pale, empty shades, bewildered, incoherent. They appear much more up in this world than in their own. They seem intensely anxious to establish their own identity, and recall most trivial details. They say and do the most inexplicable things; but give no real glimpse of the hereafter.

"But Messrs. Myers, Hodgson, and William James, being earnest inquirers of mediums (on earth), are now themselves in the next world, and know all.

F. W. H. Myers and "Katie King"

"A month after F. W. H. Myers' death he spoke, and (in one thing) was not changed. *He at once told them to take notes!* But he seemed dazed. He had forgotten the Society of Psychical Research (of which he had been President, and where he did so much work)! When first dead he thought he was in a strange town (on earth), and was groping about."

"Katie King," Sir Wm. Crookes' materialised spirit from the other world, never uttered one word of its secrets, or told us a single new thing about it during the years she visited him!

One spirit says, speaking of Spiritist revelations: "All will be destroyed that is believed by the Church, but, at the same time, the spirits have nothing to tell us that was not declared by Jesus!"

This absurd statement is equally false in all its parts. The Church and Christ are not thus mutually destructive, and all that "Raymond" says, as well as all the statements of the rest of the spirits, with the exception, as we shall see, of those who spoke through a few pious mediums, is precisely what "was *not* declared by Jesus."

Mr. Stead and "Julia"

Respecting God, the utterances of whoever spoke through Mr. Stead (who was at any rate a reverent believer in Scripture), whether "Julia" (Miss Julia Ames), or himself, are most beautiful. I will give an example or two, just to show that Stead's "other world" is at the very opposite pole from Raymond's; and it seems too great a strain to believe that both records are true! Stead says:—

"The whole difference in Heaven is that we live in love. We live in misery now; but God is love, and the law of spiritual growth. Christ is Incarnate Divinity, and we are one army of the living God.

"Don't cross God out of your life. All round man lies the quickening Spirit of God. All earthly words fail to describe the love of God. The ozone of our life is love. God has not left man in darkness, nor has He given a misleading light.

"I was not a saint nor an angel," says "Julia" (showing angels are distinct to her). "We live in the very love of God. We bring with us all our moral diseases, but get cured here. Souls need a Saviour and a Deliverer.

"In my Lord dwells all the fullness of the Godhead

bodily; God is love, and love to me. Heaven is full of Christ, and the bliss of seeing Him."

Confusion of Spiritism

I do not say there is anything new to Christian ears in all this; but we can certainly feel we are in a Christian atmosphere, very different from that of Mrs. Piper or Eusapia Palladino. Here we are, at any rate, taught that God is a person, and pervades heaven. Elsewhere in Spiritism we are taught, with equal assurance: (1) that everything is God (*pantheism*); (2) that there is no God (*atheism*); and (3) that we are God (*modernism*).

The plain man gets rather impatient with such confusion, and I think most will agree with me that, in the reconstruction which is now everywhere in the air, not the least important item is the return of the nation to a belief in the Word of God, that impregnable rock of Holy Scripture, of which Christ Himself declared: "Heaven and earth shall pass away, but My words shall not pass away."

Great Need of Clear Thinking

Why, at the present moment, a vast number will probably even rather believe the marvels recorded in this book, with all its faults and possible errors, and written by a busy physician, than the marvels of the Bible is inexplicable; and, more wondrous still, sane men and women (called by some "thoughtful") actually place more faith in the incoherent contra-dictions of Spiritism than in the sublime authori-tative utterances of the Bible respecting the other world. The "sanity" that shows such credulity does not seem to include "clear thinking."

Let me here remind my readers that no amount of moving or floating of furniture, etc., reveals anything of another world; and that even the materialisation of "spirits" is no proof of anything respecting the dead, as it occurs with the living as well, as recorded in that remarkable work "Phantasms of the Living." The following instance, well known to myself, will explain what I mean.

W. T. Stead and Mrs. Morris

Mrs. Morris, who was Mr. Stead's right hand, and who wrote all those cheap abridgments of popular works that used to be so conspicuous on our bookstalls, lived in Bayswater, and was constantly under my eye. She had, however, never been to Wimbledon, though so often pressed to go by Mr. Stead, who lived there. One Sunday morning, at church there, to the amazement and delight of Mr. Stead, in walked the very well-known figure of Mrs. Morris, with her enormous and unmistakable picture-hat that was common talk all over Bayswater. He watched her go up the aisle to a front seat, and never took his eyes off her, noticing particularly that she found she had no money in her pocket for the offertory. At the close of the service she rose before the others, and passed down the aisle, followed closely by Mr. Stead, who wanted her to come to lunch; but when he got outside she had vanished. He went immediately to the station, but she never came there.

On Monday morning he went to Bayswater to know

why she had evaded him, only to find she had been in bed three days with bronchitis, and her mother, in attendance, declared Mrs. Morris had never left her room. Mr. Stead was not the man to let matters rest here, but went off at once to the S.P.R. and enlisted the services of the late Mr. Frank Podmore. He went down to Wimbledon, and came to Bayswater, and interviewed all sorts of people, and, finally, wrote his conclusion, which certainly did not satisfy Mr. Stead: "That it was quite established that Mrs. Morris had attended the morning service at Wimbledon Church that morning; and also that, at the same time, she was in her bed in Bayswater; but, inasmuch as a person could not be in two places at the same time, there must be some mistake somewhere!"

Hasty Theories Condemned

It is only when the reader has read "Phantasms of the Living" that he discovers this class of case is too common and well evidenced to be dismissed as being all mistakes. I quite grant that all true materialisations are, in the present state of our knowledge, not wholly explicable; but I submit that, if our grandfathers had been told that the point of a steel needle, pressing into a groove in a revolving hard vulcanite disc, would produce, not a scratching sound, but the blending in perfect harmony of four voices at the same moment, or the simultaneous sounds of the various instruments in a full brass band, they would with one consent have declared it, not only inexplicable, but impossible, and ourselves rather daring liars. It might happen, therefore,

amid so many marvels, that the secret of materialisation may yet be fully revealed, without our having
hasty recourse to "spirit" theories. Once more,
then, let me emphasise the fact that no theories of
another world can be based on physical phenomena,
and that the doctrines of Spiritism, such as they
are, rest on the supposed objective communications
received through mediums and otherwise.

"Julia" Reflects Stead's Mind

But to return, and continue our epitome of the
Spiritist presentment of the other world. Mr. Stead,
in speaking further of the departed, is equally devout,
though hardly so orthodox. He says (or, rather, the
spirit speaking through him): "All the saved and
lost meet a message of love and mercy when they
die; but some know Christ not, and the lost see Him
not." "There are three essentials to see the eternal
realities: the heart of a child, keen common-sense,
and patience." How intensely "W. T. Steadish"
all these communications are, and what a gulf between
them and others we shall quote from the same
Spiritist faith! Truly, in this case, from the same
fountain come sweet waters and bitter!

As to locale, we are told by one spirit the other
world is on the earth just where we are; by another
that it is beyond the Milky Way—a distance so
remote that, travelling at twelve million miles a
minute, it would take some 15,000 *years* to reach!

Assured Conviction of Spiritism

Sir Oliver Lodge seems to know more than most
about this mysterious region, and, in "Christopher,"

a recent book (p. 61), speaks as follows: "In the light of this assured conviction of Spiritism*. . . how impious appears the attitude of those who, dominated by priestcraft, seek anxiously to know the fate of their departed, torment themselves with hopes and fears, question whether they are saved, and endeavour to convince themselves that (their) eternal fate is settled once and for ever. . . at the instant of death." "Impious" is distinctly bold; though, if one may suggest it to Sir Oliver, hardly descriptive of those who hold the faith he so strongly condemns. The impious, on the contrary so far as we know, hold no such tenets, and, as a rule, are quite indifferent to the whole subject.

"Christopher"

For something a little more positive let us turn over the leaves of "Christopher" (Sir Oliver Lodge) a little further, to page 254. Here F. W. H. Myers, speaking now from the other world, says: "Firstly and chiefly, I see ground to believe that the state of the dead is one of endless evolution . . . their loves of earth persist . . . the communion of saints . . . constitutes the life everlasting. Even our loving memory . . . supports . . . these delivered spirits upon their upward way. No wonder, since we are to them but as fellow-travellers, shrouded in a (earthly) mist. 'Neither death nor life, nor height nor depth,

* But, alas! Spiritism has no assured convictions, as I feel certain Sir Oliver well knows, but is one mass of contradictions. One would have hoped that the bathos of Raymond about the next world, published shortly before, would have now suggested silence about it as more suitable.

nor any other creature can *bar us from the hearth
fires of the universe.'* "

We leave the reader to choose between the bathos
of this appalling misquotation and the true conclusion of St. Paul—"can separate us from the love
of God, which is in Christ Jesus our Lord." Strange
and piteous that the gifted author of that wonderful
poem "St. Paul" should have had so little respect
to its subject, and should have so lowered his own
great fame when in the other world, where, at any
rate, we expect some spiritual advance!*

Seven Spheres of Theosophy

After death, we are told, there are seven stages of
progress through the seven revolving spheres of
Raymond, who himself is in the third of these.

When we turn to Mr. A. P. Sinnett, the well-known
Theosophist, we find this, and much more, is Theosophy, pure and simple. He says: "In the next
world people seem in Spiritism mainly desirous of
reaffirming the familiar truth, that to be happy hereafter, we must be decently well-behaved in this
life—a warning which, as a rule, makes no deep
impression on the hearers."

Speaking of the "seven planes," he says: "There
are the astral and manasic and other planes, the
ultimate being Karma.

"The astral region is a huge hollow sphere (not a
ring) surrounding the physical globe, like the atmosphere, and revolving with it round the sun.

"A great part of the spheres is submerged

* Such a bathos is surely enough to any who knew F. W. H.
Myers to show the words were none of his!

beneath the solid crust of the earth; here only the very lowest people are found. The lowest plane of the seven is terrible, so is the second; the third is just above the surface of the earth, and there is great discomfort; the fourth is the first of happiness; the fifth is intellectual happiness; the sixth is spiritual happiness; the seventh is perfect happiness. There are seven rulers of these spheres of high character."

Personally I have had nightmares not so bad as this concept of the Theosophic future!

More of Julia Ames

A few more extracts from Julia Ames will be an agreeable antidote here.*

As we have seen, her spiritual (rather than "Spiritist") letters describe Heaven largely from the Christian point of view, with, however, some differences. Her beings don't eat and drink, like Raymond's, but are clothed with immortal youth, and are ever in the presence of the Lord.

"Peace, joy, and love is the atmosphere of Heaven. We are lost in love. We know of the sin and sorrow you of earth suffer. There is a Hell here; but it is the joy of Heaven to be always emptying Hell"(!) A much later letter says: "Hell is a great remedial agency. The punishment

* I may, perhaps, mention that, having one day incautiously expressed to Mr. Stead my approval of some of "Julia's" beautiful descriptions of the love of God, I was immediately, without my consent, to my great annoyance, made a "Companion of the Rosary of Julia," and presented with a book of her "spirit" revelations. Only now, in these pages, do I resume my acquaintance with this mythical being after nearly thirty years.

of sin is remedial. No great gulf is fixed between Heaven and Hell. (Bible students will note this correction of our Lord's words.) The sinner is unable to save himself, and undo the consequences of his sins." "Money, rank, merit, privilege, are nothing here. The old Hell is abolished; but there is a real Hell; and you make your next life day by day (on earth). We have not yet attained; we press forward still. My Guide has been my Guardian angel in my earthly life. On Christmas Day, 1894, my Guide and I flew through space. We were oppressed by the illimitable of the universe. The motion was not flying, it was by thought. Then we approached the world of bliss; and here I met friends." "Am I now a demon or a familiar spirit? No. But evil agencies exist."

Hell

Respecting Hell, the disembodied spirit of Samuel Wilberforce, Bishop of Winchester, on July 21st, 1871, through the Rev. Stainton Moses, is said to have described Hell in similar terms to the above.

"Julia" seems to represent the transition stage of Hell, between that of an earlier date, and the later Spiritists. Emanuel Swedenborg, in an earlier age, was a great materialist as to the other world. Nevertheless, he found a Hell, and all the sects who differed from his own were there in endless punishment!

Now, based on Theosophy (of which "Julia" herself shows no trace), there is no Hell. All are immortal, and rise by six or seven steps to Karma, through as many concentric spheres. After death (not as the resurrection—which is now abolished) a spiritual body is at once received—an exact counterpart of the old. "*The sense of need supplies clothes when they are required.*" "There is gradual and interminable progress in the next world."

"All spirits in the other world are nothing else but the souls of those who have lived here" ("Spiritism Unveiled," D. L. Lanslots, p. 36).*

"Our guides are neither male nor female. We assume the bodies of children, and other forms, to gain recognition."

"The bodies of animals are material, as on earth, but nearer the human form (!); and they perform manual labour as servants."†

Banalities from "Raymond"

I trust I shall not be accused of irreverence if I close with a few of Raymond's sketches of "the other side." My apology (for I feel one is needed) for so doing is the world-wide reputation of the book, owing chiefly to the high standing of its author. I will be very brief, and as little offensive as possible.

So far as I can discover, Raymond's Heaven is only for well-educated persons of good disposition; I can discover no "lower classes." He lives in a real street, wears real clothes, and has a real dog (scientists may cavil at the word "real"); and yet can pass in an instant from Heaven (wherever it may be) and stand behind Sir Oliver Lodge's chair in his house at Edgbaston.

* All other spirits, as well as the Devil, are thus excluded.

† This concept of semi-human cats, dogs, horses, etc., as servants is as grotesque as it is uncanny. "Manual labour" is also very funny.

"All is solid (another poser) in the next world. There is mud (of all things) in Heaven, and there are bricks—real bricks. The houses on the other side are built of these! The ground is solid, and if you kneel in the mud you soil your clothes"* (p. 184†). "Something chemical rises from the earth (this Heaven, then, can't be far off) that makes solid trees and flowers." Raymond has all his earthly occupations. He attends lectures, goes to church, where there are real pews, and where (save the mark!) he dozes—an indication, I fear, of the dullness of celestial discourses. He is not always in uniform. "Fancy me," he says, "in white robes."

The Travesty of Heaven

Raymond's body is like what he had before. In Heaven the blind receive their sight, and cripples have new limbs. "If, however, you have been blown to pieces," Raymond says, "it takes (naturally) some time to form the spirit body" (see p. 189). Cigars (of some tobacco substitute) are made there; and whisky (of some sort) can be procured! (p. 195). "There are dogs, cats and other animals there." "We have books, but are not too serious." "We dance, cake-walk, and are full of jokes!" (p. 213).

But one must stop quoting this, to me, somewhat

---

* For what reason are these absurd banalities printed? They serve no purpose of identification, which is usually their excuse! The whole seems a cruel attempt to bring Sir Oliver Lodge's deserved reputation itself down into the mud!

† These references are to Sir Oliver Lodge's book "Raymond."

nauseous and revolting twaddle. I know I shall be decried, for such words, as a partisan, as a wolf in sheep's clothing, as one pretending to write a fair book on a great subject, and yet descending to the coarsest abuse, etc.; but I ask, in the name of decency and common sense, "What am I to say?

"Raymond," Science and Religion

Once more I acknowledge the profound self-sacrifice of the great scientist in publishing such a book; but can I believe he has been well advised in doing so? No, a thousand times no! If a father must listen (with infinite pain) to a "Feda" (the supposed spirit of a little ignorant Indian girl speaking through some medium), in the hope of catching the loved tones of a dear son, at any rate let the privacy of the whole subject be respected, and the veil closely drawn over such extraordinary revelations. Surely any scientist must know that no respectable "science" can be benefited by the publication of such absurd utterances!

If any wish to take the one step that is said to cover the distance from the sublime to the ridiculous, let them first peruse the fifteenth chapter of St. Paul's first letter to the Corinthians and then a chapter of "Raymond."

I think, brief and discursive as I have been, I have shown the highest and the lowest (Spiritist) ideas of the other world; but I feel I should add that the lofty views of "Julia," so far as I can find, are endorsed by no other Spiritist whatever, the future world developed by the rank and file of Spiritists being clearly Theosophic.

The Weakest Point

And now to sum up very briefly the situation so far as we have got. The evidence of Spiritism concerning another world is its weakest point. If we deduct from its utterances all that is clearly a repetition of Theosophic imaginations, we have actually nothing coherent left. There is a mass, of which I have given a fair sample, of detached and contradictory statements presenting no mental picture of anything. It is certainly incredible, if there be any communications from the dead, that none of whose whole earthly lives were spent on this very problem, and who specially arranged when they "passed over" to give full revelations—such as Myers, Hodgson, Professor James, and others— should say anything but what is certainly more like the outcome of the medium's mind than of their own.

No Messages from the Dead

After fifty years of these revelations *nothing is revealed;* our thirst for such knowledge remains absolutely unquenched. Modern Spiritism set out with high hopes and promises, which, so far, have not been realised. Respecting the mere fact of other intelligences and powers than our own, I should say it has been established; but that these are the spirits of the departed dead seems negatived by the character of their utterances.

Mr. Birrell, at Bristol, said: "The records of Spiritism leave me unconvinced. They lack the things of morality, of grandeur, of emotion; in a word, of religion. They deal with petty things, mere prolonged egoism, as if the one thing we want to be assured of is continued existence, and an endless capacity to exchange platitudes. A revelation of the life beyond the grave ought surely, if it is to do any good in the world, to be more stupendous than that—something of really first-class importance. Otherwise we are just as well without it."

When we consider the enormous benefit supposed to be conferred on our race by the establishing of the mere fact of a spirit world to those who believe the truth of Spiritist statements, we must not forget that, if these members of our race had thought the word of the Lord Himself as worthy of belief as that of Spiritists, they would have required no further evidence. Those who believe the Bible, indeed, know far more of the other world than ever Raymond or Myers have revealed in their utterances.

Any further explanations of the real source of the messages recorded here will be found in the next two chapters.

CHAPTER V

EXPLANATIONS OF SPIRITIST PHENOMENA

Money and Fraud

Spiritist "truths" seem to differ from all others in requiring a special atmosphere, a special attitude, special apparatus, and special preparation to demonstrate them. Even when all has been carefully arranged no truth may be demonstrated, and nothing whatever may happen at the séance. And then comes the almost irresistible opening for fraud and trickery. For here are some sixty people or more waiting to see something for which they have paid, and the mysterious power is absent to-day. One of two things must be done. A reason must be found for the failure—the presence of even one sceptic will do nicely—but then the money should be returned; or fraudulent phenomena (very easy to produce) must be shown, when, of course, the money is safe. Some mediums will adopt one course, and some the other. All one can say is that in public séances—in America more than in Europe—some sort of fraud is the rule, and not the exception; and so also in all private séances where money is paid. Where it is not paid, fraud is rarer, but not unknown.

The "Electric Fluid"

The séance is probably opened with prayer and always continued with hymns, more or less flavoured with negroes and revivals (seldom including those of the class of "Ancient and Modern"). These are supposed to produce a good atmosphere of an elevated character and to invoke good spirits. The general experience, however, is that all this soon degenerates to folly or evil. Folly seems as inseparable from a Spiritist séance as fraud; and both are most objectionable. Hands are then joined and under no circumstances may they be unclasped for one moment, as the "electrical fluid" that helps to materialise the spirit form absolutely depends on an unbroken ring. All this is solemnly impressed upon the audience. A humble member, however, once (not the only occasion) loosed one of her hands, and so broke the current of "electrical fluid;" but all went on just the same without a hitch!*

Seeing is Believing

It is doubtful whether any who have not actually seen the phenomena can believe in their reality, for our reason is decidedly against the possibility of their occurrence. They are only established on the evidence of one's own sense at first hand, and in spite of all logic. Nothing but direct unmistakable evidence can convince; in short, one must be an eye-witness. If one may allude to it in such doubtful connection, it was only in this way the actual resurrection of our Lord was established, and the

* There is, however, much psychological force in these hymns and joined hands, which I will speak of in Chapter IX.

attitude of those who only *hear* of these marvels is very like that taken by St. Thomas of old: "Except I see, I will not believe." The failure of many scientists who have sought to investigate the subject, and who have failed to witness any phenomena, is probably due, not to any particular fault, or lack of earnest preparation on the part of the medium, but to a want of knowledge of the laws (as yet unknown) that produce such phenomena.

The Docile Audience

Generally the audience is in a most receptive and accommodating mood. They have been carefully instructed before that it is only in this condition that they can expect to see that for which they have paid their money; and if they indulge a critical or sceptical spirit, they need not be surprised if they go empty away.

Dr. Lappius, in "Hypnotism and Spiritism," says: "Another simple fact is the facility with which the spirits seem to adapt themselves to the tastes, prejudices, and beliefs of their clients."

On the other hand, it must be conceded that most sitters find it easiest to attribute anything they may see or hear, to that which is in accordance with the Spiritist doctrine at the séance.

Dobson has shown that this doctrine practically depends on three hypotheses: (1) There is a spirit world. (2) Departed souls can be spoken to. (3) The medium is a necessary link between the two worlds.

Psychology of Mediums

This brings us again to these extraordinary beings, for there is no doubt they are out of the ordinary. Any one cannot be a medium, but a great many more could be if they were aware of the power they possess. A well-known Christian doctor discovered one of his servant-maids had these powers to an extraordinary degree; and eventually she turned his house upside down with physical phenomena.*

We do not know exactly what is the peculiar psychic condition of a medium. It appears to be, so far as I can judge, some state akin to auto-hypnotism, or, to use inexact, old-fashioned language, "self-mesmerism," during which the unconscious mind, usually buried in the deepest obscurity "below the threshold," is brought into prominence and dominance, while the conscious mind is in abeyance and not used, as in hypnotism. With most mediums this results in an apparent "trance" condition of unconsciousness; but others do not appear to be wholly asleep or unconscious (as in modern hypnotism), but reach the same condition. There is a great tendency for professional hypnotic subjects to become mediums.

It must be borne in mind that those who alone, in their rooms, get direct writing or raps are themselves mediums, though at first they may not have known their powers.

The medium is always exhausted by her efforts, sometimes to a dangerous extent. As I have said elsewhere, the power is seldom lifelong; in Stainton

* See p. 39.

Moses it extended over eleven years. It may go suddenly or gradually.

I have also pointed out that the term "medium" is objectionable, as it assumes the very point which has to be proved.

No Test Conditions

Important séances are very different to-day from what they were some years ago. They are now conducted under the most rigid test conditions, and fraud is difficult.

But in every experiment before Sir. Wm. Crookes, D. D. Home, dictated the whole conditions of the séance; and Stainton Moses, to mention the two who were by far the most celebrated and most reliable mediums forty years ago and have never been equalled since, also worked in complete darkness, unbound, without tests or precautions of any kind, and in the midst of a circle of confiding friends; and the phenomena were generally reported by himself.*

No doubt conjuring could explain some of the lesser physical phenomena, but not all. It must ever be remembered that a medium, unlike a conjurer, if she finds the conditions too hard, can remain passive and produce nothing, without any discredit.

Eusapia Palladino

Mrs. Piper and Eusapia Palladino were the two most celebrated and trustworthy mediums during the last thirty years. A committee of the S.P.R. went to Italy to test Eusapia, and reported well of

* F. Podmore, "The Newer Spiritism," p. 149.

her, but Mr. Frank Podmore was not satisfied with the ordinary physical phenomena he witnessed.

One day Eusapia had Sir Oliver Lodge, F. W. H. Myers, and Ochovowicz as audience, and, during some raps, was discovered making them herself by striking her boot on the floor; and yet she seemed quite unconscious of the fact.* But, on December 18th, 1911, a young man hid himself in Eusapia's cabinet, and suddenly grasped her left foot, which at that moment (so far as he knew) was pressing hard on Professor Münsterberg's boot. She was also convicted of fraud at other times.

There are further details about mediums which tend to show that, however true their motives, however good their object, the fact of laying their minds voluntarily open to spirit influences in this way is fraught with danger, not only mental and moral, but also actually physical. There are also terrible stories about mediums, all of which cannot be doubted, respecting these latter risks.

Sir Wm. Barrett, alluding to the above, says: "Granting the existence of the spirit world, it is necessary to be on one's guard against the invasion of our will (when so surrendered) by a lower order of intelligence and morality."

Scientific Tests

There can be no doubt, turning to proved phenomena, that the man who denies them is not entitled to be called a scientist; he is simply ignorant. There are, however, in the scientific world still a

---

* Practically it is most difficult to prove how far *conscious* fraud extends; there is such a mixture.

large class of robust, though not very acute, intellects who in former days long affirmed that hypnotism, telepathy, wireless telegraphy, etc., were all unscientific and unproved balderdash. Now they say the same respecting the proved facts of Spiritism.[*]

Not that any of these proofs reach the standard of what Sir Wm. Crookes indicated was the only way in which supernatural powers could be proved. As a *scientific observer*, he asks that some additional weight be deposited in one pan of his balance when the case is locked; as a *chemist*, he asks for one-thousandth part of a grain of arsenic to be placed in a hermetically sealed glass tube of distilled water. No such proofs of supernatural power have been given anywhere during the last 100 years.

Proved Facts

Nevertheless, in Professor Bottazzi's physiological laboratory, at Naples, when the doors were padlocked and sealed, the Professor has seen various human limbs appear, hands in great activity which worked apparatus, and all sorts of clothing apparently produced out of nothing. A professor of astronomy observes, with regard to spirit phenomena, that the facts must either be admitted as proved, or the possibility of certifying any facts by human tests must be given up.

Sir Wm. Barrett ("On the Threshold of the Unseen," p. 98) says: "Of the real objective exist-

[*] Helmholtz said to Sir Wm. Barrett that neither the evidence of all the members of the Royal Society nor of his own senses would ever make him believe in thought-transference; yet this is now proved and generally accepted.

ence of most of these supernormal phenomena, the evidence appears to me to be overwhelming."

Professor Henry Sidgwick says: "It is a scandal that any dispute as to the reality of any of the marvellous phenomena of Spiritism should still be going on."

Investigation

The three who investigated Eusapia's wonderful physical phenomena at Naples were Mr. Baggally, a most expert professional conjurer, who after thirty-five years had never seen one genuine physical phenomenon; Mr. Feilden, Secretary of the S.P.R., who for ten years had never seen one genuine physical phenomenon; and Mr. H. Carrington, who for twelve years had exposed all Spiritist frauds in the U.S.A., and had also never seen one genuine phenomenon in their séances! In December, 1908, these three clever sceptics had eleven sittings with Eusapia, and were absolutely convinced of the genuineness of the physical phenomena shown.

Sir Wm. Crookes (quoted by R. J. Thompson, in "Proofs of Life after Death," p. 73) says: "That certain physical phenomena, such as the movement of material substances, and the production of sounds resembling electric discharges (raps), occur under circumstances in which they cannot be explained by any physical laws at present known, is a fact of which I am as certain as I am of the most elementary fact of chemistry. My whole scientific education has been one long lesson in exactness of observation; and I wish it to be distinctly understood that this firm conviction is the result of most careful investigations."

Established Phenomena

Sir William Crookes regards the following as proved certainties:—

1. *Heavy bodies are moved without contact.* The force, which is very great, seems to be directed by spirit intelligence.

2. *Sounds produced without visible agency.* These are very common and significant.

3. *Heavy bodies move to order,* in any way, without contact.

4. *Levitation of articles* (of furniture) without contact.

5. *Levitation of human beings.* He has seen a lady sitting on a chair raised eight inches off the ground.*

6. (Rapid) *movements of small articles* (such as small musical instruments, toys, flowers, ribbons, letters, etc., which fly through the air in all directions).

7. *Alteration in weight.* Sir William Crookes has seen articles placed on the weighing machine apparently increase in weight from 8 to 43, 46, and 48 lbs.

8. *Luminous appearances* (often intensely vivid).

9. *The appearance of human hands* (and other limbs, often very active).

10. *Direct writing.* In this the pencil moves and writes of its own accord, no one being within a foot of the table; and sometimes the bottom sheet of a packet of notepaper is written on without visible pencil.†

---

* In addition to others recorded in Chapter III.

† In automatic writing the fingers twitch and itch, and you feel you must put pen to paper, and then "it" writes in a firm, clear hand, entirely independently of your will. You never

11. *Phantom forms and faces*. This includes all materialisations, such as "Katie King," whom Sir William Crookes saw, and examined, and spoke to, on and off, for three years.

Incontestable Evidence

Long afterwards, as President of the British Association in 1898, Sir William said: "Thirty years ago I published an account of experiments tending to show that, outside our scientific knowledge, *there exists a force* exercised by intelligence differing from the ordinary intelligence common to mortals."

Sir Oliver Lodge points out, in this connection, that "an affirmation from his own experience by the humblest man is worth listening to; whereas the denial, *in his ignorance*, of the cleverest is not worth a moment's attention."

Another scientist says: "A large proportion of the phenomena are genuine, and are directed by some non-human intelligence."

M. Maeterlinck truly says: "Raps and marvels of untouched tables, the transportation of articles without contact, human phenomena and materialisations, are as incontestable as polarisation or crystallisation; or else we must abandon all human certainty. Levitation seems not quite so certain. This unknown power lifts tables, moves the heaviest articles, produces flowers and hair (from nowhere),

know when the impulse may come (as in speaking with "tongues"). It comes suddenly and goes suddenly and may or may not be accompanied by raps. Dr. Marcel Violett says, "When the medium writes it is mechanical and automatic, not intellectual. Another personality writes and may speak through the medium." This is of great importance.

plays on strings and notes, passes through solid matter, conjures up ghosts, and makes lights—all on one condition, 'That all performances must be, without rhyme or reason, vain and puerile!'"*

Some Unknown Force

So far, then, we have as clear proof as can possibly be afforded of some force, at present unknown to us, used by non-human intelligences; but, so far as we can see, for absolutely silly and purposeless follies. To account for all this, the old "dæmons," a freakish race of spirits (not of the dead), have been revived. These were once everywhere believed in, though not revealed to us definitely in the Bible. They are supposed to be intermediate between the good and fallen angels, inclining to evil, however, rather than to good. The only suggestions of this existence are these, and other purposeless and foolish displays of power when invoked. Of these there are, of course, other explanations.

Still, the more we investigate these phenomena, the less, in one sense, we seem to know.

With regard to spirit photography, while it cannot be wholly denied, it is best to exclude it from the above category, as it is so easy to imitate.

We may emphasize once more that all these physical phenomena have no *necessary* connection whatever with the dead.

Professor Hyslop insists that all physical phenomena must be excluded at once, as not in themselves in any respect affording evidence of the actions of departed spirits.

* This remark seems very well justified.

Attempted Explanations

The full explanation of these extraordinary physical freaks is confessedly impossible. I will, however, produce what attempts have been made to do so. First of all, undoubtedly, stand the psycho-dynamic theory of Thomas Jay Hudson, the American scientist.

Taking the medium's powers as essentially an activity of the powers of the unconscious mind, he says these are three in number:—

1. Intuition, or instinct.
2. Telepathy.
3. Telekinesis, or the power to move physical objects at a distance by mind power alone without contact.

It is this third that constitutes psycho-dynamics. Hudson, therefore, accounts for Spiritist physical phenomena by the unconscious mind of the medium possessing physical power to make itself felt (and heard), to move ponderable objects, without visible contact, and to order.

No Proof of Psycho-Dynamics

The great objection to this admirable theory, which explains everything with perfect ease, is not only that there is no proof whatever of anything at all resembling "telekinesis," apart from electricity of some sort, but that the very concept does violence to our ideas of the distinct and different character of force in the spirit and in the material worlds, and seems to confuse both. We must note that our spirits can move our bodies by our own will only while there is living contact; for, even if a limb be still attached to the body, if living contact with the brain be broken, as in paralysis, the leg or arm will no longer respond to the will. There is no ground for believing that disembodied spirits, at any rate, can move any object whatever, so that the force in physical phenomena, whatever it be, does not come from them.

Sir Wm. Barrett very properly remarks that he cannot conceive how intelligence can act on matter.

"Raymond," as we have seen, is simpler in his explanation, and prefers the venerable chestnut that "all the circle supply 'magnetism,' which is gathered by the medium, and goes into the table, and we manipulate it" (p. 144).

After all, one explanation seems almost as intelligible as the other!

Other Unproved Theories

Materialisation is also accounted for by Professor Morselli on the psycho-dynamic theory, which, he says, is the only alternative to the "spirits." Others speak mysteriously of "compressed" and "impressed" ether, and declare the "astral body" is nothing else than "condensed" ether, and that ether can produce materialisation (and a heart beating at 75?). Of course, the very existence of ether has still to be postulated, being not yet proved, and the compression or condensing of a substance 1,000 times denser than steel is at least difficult to grasp.

Rev. A. Chambers has a theory of his own: "A spirit materialises from the aura, which is matter in a fluid condition, as it exhales from the physical bodies" (of the sitters?), "and consolidates round the spirit-self, forming a temporary physical encasement" (with legs that can move, and a voice that can speak?).

Let us agree, rather than commit ourselves to any of the above solutions, in the statement that "we don't know how it's done."

Personally, I've never seen a conjurer yet where I haven't had to say this; so it's nothing new, I suspect, to most of us; nor is it even very surprising, that we have yet to wait for the full solution of some undoubted facts.

Explanation of Psychic Phenomena

Leaving these perplexing physical phenomena alone for the present, we will proceed to consider the alleged communications supposed to come from another world, received by raps, which spell out words, or by writing by the medium's hand, or wholly independently and automatically, and by slate writing.

I have pointed out it is these phenomena alone that constitute any evidence of another world. Those who deny another world *in toto* find their only explanation of psychic phenomena in telepathy, a very recently discovered science, but one which is now of fair respectability in the scientific world. According to Mr. Frank Podmore, telepathy is the only thing in Spiritist phenomena that is established as a scientific fact beyond all doubt.   Sir Oliver Lodge says: "The facts of telepathy must be regarded as practically established in the judgment of those who have studied them."

Telepathy

To account for the marvels of mediums, however, the powers of this telepathy have to be stretched to their utmost possible bounds, and, some think, beyond them. I will explain what I mean. The ordinary and simplest meaning of telepathy is the transference of conscious thought without words; but this by no means suffices here, for the medium often makes allusions to facts unknown (consciously) to any of the audience. It is, therefore, suggested, not without reason, that the powers of telepathy (here really including psychometry) enable the medium, not only to reproduce the thought of the hearers, but the stores of memory in their unconscious minds, in which lie buried (as has been scientifically proved by Dr. Milne Bramwell and others) innumerable thoughts and facts quite out of consciousness. Of course, it is the medium's own unconscious mind that has this power, and, therefore, only in a state of trance can this be done. Perhaps a few words from others will make this clearer.

Powers of the Unconscious Mind

F. W. H. Myers says: "My work on 'Human Personality'" (two big volumes) "is in large measure a critical attack upon the main Spiritist position; the belief, namely, that 'all or almost all super-normal phenomena are due to the action of the spirits of the departed dead.' It has been suggested that *in every case the supposed spirit 'control' is none other than the medium's own unconscious mind.*"

In Spiritist telepathy, then, it is probably the

unconscious mind of the medium that reads that of the inquirer, where all is buried. The "spirit," therefore, that mostly "controls" the medium appears to be her own unconscious mind (subliminal consciousness); and not Feda, Moonstone, &c.

Thomas Jay Hudson plainly says: "No facts not known by telepathy can be communicated by mediums. When the unconscious mind obtains control of the planchette, it writes what is quite unknown to the writer's conscious mind, and which is, therefore, attributed to the dead; for by far the larger proportion, as I hold, of the messages are due to the activity of the still-embodied spirit of the medium."

Cryptomnesia

C. E. Hudson, in the *Nineteenth Century* for May, 1919, p. 906, says: "In *very* few cases can subconscious telepathy be finally ruled out as a possible explanation of the automatic writing."

Facts are read by the medium's unconscious mind which are buried in the unconscious memories of the hearers, and of which no one in the room is consciously aware. Of course, this assumes the fact of cryptomnesia, or the hidden unconscious memory.*

An extraordinary example of cryptomnesia is recorded by Maeterlinck in "Our Eternity." Col. de Rochas can hypnotise exceptional subjects and make them re-enact scenes from youth up. He took Josephine, a girl of eighteen, back to a baby at her mother's breast; then he takes her back before her birth; and then comes the voice of an old man,

---

* This can be easily demonstrated by closely studying a page of a book for five minutes and then closing it. The conscious mind can then repeat a few lines; slight hypnosis brings as much again; and deep hypnosis may recall the whole page.

whose name is Jean Claude Burdon. He is bed-
ridden. He was born in 1812, and gives his life
history, and dies at 70; and it is the dead man
speaking. He thinks he would like to be born
again; and when Josephine is born, he enters the
child's body.

Then he, in turn, is taken back to childhood,
and an old woman appears, whose name is Philomena
Carteron; she was born in 1702. And so on with
several others, back to Louis XIV. Other hypnotists
give similar stories; but it is quite possible that
Col. de Rochas and others have been hoaxed.

Telepathy in the Next World

It is generally assumed that telepathy or thought
transference largely replaces conversation in the next
world. It is also the means by which spirit messages
are received; for it is not by actual speech, but by
thought transference, that the "spirits" communicate their information.

Kant records the discovery by Swedenborg of a
lost receipt in a secret drawer by direction of a
deceased husband. This is supposed to be due to
"deferred telepathy." (See Sir Oliver Lodge,
"Survival of Man," p. 120.)

Dr. Osty (see Maeterlinck) had all the leading
events of his life for three years told to him—as
we now know—by telepathy. The forty volumes of
these experiments of the S.P.R. have fully established
their new power as a scientific fact.

Before the S.P.R.'s investigations clairvoyance,
telepathy, and hypnotism (when not frauds) were
all thought to be supernatural. It is not so now.

Telepathy Does Not Account for All

But, on the other hand, Alfred Russel Wallace says: "The scientific world has been proved to have been totally wrong in its denial of the facts of psychic phenomena; and to call the subjective unconscious mind the sole author of these phenomena is as unscientific as attributing them to spirit agency." (And yet, surely, these are our only alternatives.)

Stainton Moses (1897) supports this: "These five years the messages you have received may, as you suggest, have been due solely to your own sub-consciousness. Your hand may have been moved (in writing) by some part of your own soul! Well, be it so, if you please." Again, another scientist says: "There is a sufficient basis for a reasonable *belief* in the existence of disembodied minds. There is, however, no *proof*, even by 'cross-correspond-ence,' of such disembodied minds; but they are suggested, though not conclusively, because of the possibility of telepathy from living minds."

One of the "spirits" says: "You need not disturb yourself about whether it all comes from me, or from your own sub-conscious self."

Myers, Hodgson, James

"There are many cases," says Myers, "with Mrs. Piper that cannot be explained by any form of telepathy, unless it be so extended as to be as inconceivable as 'spirit' itself."

Yet another: "The other theory, that the mediums are governed by the unconscious mind, is impossible." And "To attempt to account by telepathy for these wonders introduces far more difficulties than it solves."

Finally, Dr. R. Hodgson is quite clear that tele-pathy does not account for Spiritist phenomena: Professor William James has also been convinced of spirit agency; while Professor C. Flammarion says, on the other hand: "After two years' investigation of automatic writing I came to the positive con-clusion that, not only are the signs *not* those of a spirit, but that the intervention of another mind from the spirit world is not proved; the fact being, the medium is more or less consciously the author of the communications by some cerebral process which yet remains to be investigated."

No Complete Solution

To me this last quotation seems a very reasonable utterance and a possible explanation of most, but not all, psychical phenomena. And yet this is not really an explanation, but simply the substitution of one mystery for another, which accounts for the interest the phenomena still excite; for once a fact, however extraordinary, is scientifically and fully explained, it ceases to interest, *e.g.*, wireless telegraphy.

Sir Wm. Crookes' *reason* declared that the pheno-mena he saw in his own house, in bright light, and with private friends only, were absolutely impossible to understand. Neither Hudson's psycho-dynamics, Professor Mayo's extra-neural theories, nor collective hypnotism (of which more anon), nor the "ectenic force" of Count de Gasparin, nor Professor Lom-broso's "psychic force," explain the phenomena.

Professor James, though his reason also revolted at what he saw, yet could not believe that the whole host of phenomena was humbug.

In "Raymond" all can be accounted for, more or less scientifically by telepathy, without the hypothesis of necromancy, with the one exception of the photograph; but can we say that even this is beyond any future possible solution?

Much Beyond our Reason

At present, we grant, there is no real explanation of the phenomenon.

Against the proposed solution by the discovery of some unknown force we would urge, no such marvels of this character have even been done before; and are we to believe that an ignorant peasant Italian woman, convicted of fraud, is such a mistress of an unknown power as to produce at will arms, hands, and feet of flesh, lights, and solid bodies of all sorts?

Once more, though we do not know the solution of all this, neither do we know how a fakir, *at will*, can weigh down 150 lbs. with a single feather placed in the other balance. Indian jugglers can produce phenomena absolutely beyond our reason; and which of us, even in England, have not seen wholly inexplicable phenomena produced by conjurers within one yard of our noses?

There remains, no doubt, the solution by the theory of another world peopled by evil spirits of all descriptions, as well as by good. Of course, to a true believer, this is no theory, but a solid fact, seeing that fortunately he *is* able to believe in the truthfulness of our Lord.

Maeterlinck's Conclusion

Respecting any solution Maeterlinck says: "If you refuse to admit the agency of spirits, the (physical) phenomena are inexplicable.

"Agreed, nor do we pretend they are not; for hardly anything is to be explained (fully) upon this earth. We are content simply to ascribe these to the incomprehensible powers of the medium.

"These singular faculties are baffling only because they are still sporadic. They are really no more marvellous than those we use daily without marvelling at them: our memory, our understanding, our imagination, and so forth. They form part of the great miracle that *we are;* and, having once admitted this miracle, we should be surprised, not so much at its extent, as at its limits.

"Nevertheless, I am not at all of opinion that we must definitely reject the spirit theory. Everything remains in suspense. Things are little removed (yet) from the point marked by Sir Wm. Crookes when he said, nearly fifty years ago (1874), in the *Quarterly Journal of Science:* 'There is no proof whatever of the agency of the spirits of the dead, though the Spiritists hold it as a faith, not demanding further proof, that the spirits of the dead are the sole agents in the production of all the phenomena.'

"Nevertheless, it is saying a good deal that recent scientific investigations have not utterly shattered the theory. But, I repeat, it is most simple to attribute these absurdities to telepathic communications."

"To whatever power these phenomena are due," continues Maeterlinck, with justifiable sarcasm, "it is quite clear it dislikes to make itself useful. It readily performs feats of sleight-of-hand, provided we can derive no profit from them. It always acts, as it were, by accident, without (apparent) reason, method, or object, in a deceitful, illogical, and preposterous fashion."

Messages Come from Spirits

F. W. H. Myers, Sir Wm. Crookes, Sir Oliver Lodge, Sir Wm. Barrett, Dr. R. Hodgson, Dr. A. R. Wallace, Professor W. James, Sir A. Conan Doyle, indeed, one might say all Modern Spiritists, are agreed that communications from spirits do at times occur.*

Of course, it is said that we believe what we desire —spirits or telepathy; nevertheless, it is in harmony with all that Christians know and believe that there is an unseen world, and beings with powers transcending our own.

The President of the S.P.R. asked, in 1910, "Are we entitled to say that Myers, being dead, yet speaketh? Personally, I am not convinced."

Professor Hyslop, after the most exhaustive study, adopts for the present the theory of spirit communication as the only sane and reasonable solution of some of the phenomena.

Professor Lombroso, in February, 1907, writes: "Spiritist phenomena are attributable to the agency of extra-terrestrial existences."

* To the Spiritist this proves "necromancy," for to him there are no spirits but those of the dead; to the Christian there are many others.

Are They Dæmons?

Sir Wm. Barrett attributes the phenomena to human-like, but not human, intelligences. They may be good or bad dæmons, but they afford no proofs of any human existence after death. He considers the only explanation of what he has witnessed is the spirit hypothesis. His words are: "Neither hallucination, imperfect or mal-observation, nor misdescription can account for the phenomena, and the simplest explanation is the spirit hypothesis."

Of these spirits Cardinal Newman writes: "Also between the hosts of evil spirits I considered there was a middle race, '*daimonia*' (dæmons), partially fallen, capricious, wayward, noble or crafty, benevolent or malicious, as the case might be."

Dr. F. van Eder, S.P.R., maintains all is the work of spirits.

After reading all these views, which I would fain were more coherent, I think we must for the present leave the riddle still unsolved.

Maeterlinck Puzzled

M. Maeterlinck is enormously puzzled with the tremendous contrast between our conscious and unconscious mind, if indeed all the absurd puerilities of Spiritism are the product of the latter and not of spirits. He asks ("The Unknown Guest"): "But how can we explain the incredible contrast between the grandeur and calmness of this inner life and the puerile and grotesque incongruities which it manifests at times? Inside us the unconscious mind is the sovereign judge, the supreme arbiter, and the prophet. In external actions (in Spiritism) it becomes somewhat of a mountebank. In one part of the world (France) it declares spirits undergo reincarnation, and tells the story of their past existence; in England, on the contrary, it generally asserts that they do not become reincarnate. It deludes itself, or it deludes us. Why does it do so? It asks for nothing, neither for money, nor prayers, nor thoughts. What is the use of these puerile pranks? It must be for the pleasure of lying; and yet I cannot believe the truth is as hideous as this. So far no conclusion can be drawn. It seems a fantastic literary exercise."

It must, of course, be remembered that the world of spirits, as revealed in the Bible, contains not only evil spirits of various orders, but those that are good and beneficent, though these latter are not much in evidence at séances. None of these, however, are the spirits of the dead.

Sceptics

We have not so far spoken of absolute sceptics in Spiritism. Sceptics, *who have inquired into it*, are not a numerous body. Faraday, a Christian Scientist, found in Spiritism nothing worthy of attention, nor any force or information of the least use or value to mankind.* Dr. A. Eulenberg says: "I am not aware of a single argument of any importance" (in favour of Spiritism). Robert Browning was the only distinguished sceptic at

* Far different is the verdict of others. The effect of Spiritism as to belief in another world on an equally distinguished man is worth noticing. Alfred Russel Wallace was a thorough sceptic and materialist, till the facts of Spiritism convinced him of the spirit universe.

D. D. Home's séances, whom he immortalised as "Sludge the Medium," a poem that might be read with some advantage by my readers.*.

I don't know that I have yet stated that Sir Wm. Crookes began his inquiry into the phenomena of Spiritism believing the whole affair was a mass of superstition and trickery; and yet, in spite of this tremendous bias, such was his honesty that he ended in staking his scientific reputation by stating "that his preconceived idea was wrong, and that a class of phenomena wholly new to science did really exist."

I hope my readers will be at least equally honest, though they may not have the same scientific reputation at stake.

The point we have arrived at is, I trust, clear. Spiritism has produced *physical* phenomena that at present cannot be entirely explained by any known force.

It has also produced *psychical* phenomena which are undoubtedly mostly caused by the medium employed.

If it be demonstrated that any of these physical or psychical phenomena are due to "spirit" agency, this does not in the least involve the action of human disembodied spirits, as there are superhuman spirits of all sorts in the other world.

* This was possibly partly written to discourage his wife, who was an ardent Spiritist.

CHAPTER VI

SPIRITISM AND THE DEAD

Proof by Assertion

As we have seen, the principal objects of Spiritism are: (1) to establish the fact of another world; (2) to prove that human life survives after death; and that (3) the dead can, and do, communicate with us (necromancy). They only succeed in absolutely establishing this third point scientifically to a minority even among their own members, and to none outside. This success, such as it is, is mostly due to a pure assumption, which they do not even attempt to prove. The assertion is that if the existence of spirits in another world can be demonstrated, these are, of necessity, the spirits of the dead, for there are none others. In support of this unwarranted statement, which flatly contradicts the Bible, and does away at once with the whole world of superhuman spirit beings, no argument is advanced, no evidence is given; it is simply asserted (after the justly condemned Hæckel method).

It is obvious that to beg the question at issue by a baseless assertion *ex cathedrâ* is a short and easy way of "proving" a point. The value of such "proof," however, is more than doubtful.

Error as to Spirits

"Spirit" to a Spiritist, but to no one else, is, therefore, necessarily synonymous with "discarnate spirit." This must be made clear, for there are many, the writer included, who dissent from it; and who believe that some of the Spiritist phenomena are due to spirit action, though not to discarnate spirits, but to those in which all Christians, and many others (as I think) rightly believe. When, therefore, others, with myself, agree that some of the physical phenomena may be due to the superhuman action of spirits, that some also of the psychical phenomena, automatic writing, etc., may be due to communications from the other world, we never refer to discarnate spirits (*i.e.*, disembodied spirits of men), but to the original denizens of the spirit world, that pervade the whole language of Scripture. No such spirit-communications have to us, therefore, any necessary connection with necromancy.

Indeed, I may point out further, that there is some important evidence on this head as to the existence of other than discarnate spirits which may not be disregarded, for it is far too well supported by evidence. As I shall show later on, we cannot believe, and in the "we" I think I may be allowed to include all Spiritists, that any human beings, however depraved, can in their spirit-form after death descend to the horrors that accompany so many cases of "possession," the secrets of so many séances. or the dreadful experiences of many Spiritists. Surely to call these denizens of the pit "discarnate spirits" is not to honour the dead, but to dishonour them, and to reach the incredible.

Humanity may descend to the bestial; but not to
the devilish, without actual "possession."

It will be understood that I do not here give the
views of individual Spiritists who may not at all
agree with the above. I think, however, it fairly
represents the general Spiritist doctrine, and the
belief of the leaders. Sir Oliver Lodge, however,
in a recent article does speak of "many grades of
development in the other world, *some lower than
humanity.*"

Is Necromancy Possible?

Bearing in mind, then, the general drift of the
above, let us consider the views for and against the
existence of the possibility and practice of necromancy in the present day.*

Those who are in favour of it, the general believers
in Spiritism, are a very numerous band,† but I think
I am quite right in saying the majority of actual
Spiritists cannot say the fact is yet absolutely
proved.

Even Sir Oliver Lodge says, "I am, for all personal
purposes, convinced of the persistence of human
existence beyond bodily death; though I am unable
to justify that belief in a full and complete manner."‡

F. W. H. Myers finds that Spiritists have proved:

* It is an error to think that the forbidding of a practice
necessarily proves its possibility. Such is not the case. It may
be forbidden, not because of its possibility, but because (as in
necromancy), the attempts bring humanity into touch with
dangerous, non-human spirits, intent on evil.

† I allude here to the audiences and camp followers of Spiritism,
and not to the small company who have studied the subject.

‡ It is, I suppose, needless to repeat that the humblest believers have known all this and more for nearly 2,000 years.

(1) Survival after death. (2) That avenues of communication between the spirit and material worlds exist. (3) That in the spirit world some memories and affections of earth persist.

Allan Kardec, founder of French Spiritism, firmly believed in communications with the dead.

Spiritists Affirm it is

Dr. Hodgson, the American representative of Spiritism, was the exposer of Madame Blavatsky, and a keen student of psychology and magic. He had Mrs. Piper under his sole charge for twenty years, and tested her in every way, as a clever psychological detective would, and believed her trustworthy. Professor Hyslop also declared her wholly trustworthy. Since Dr. Hodgson's death, Professor Hyslop, through Mrs. Piper, is satisfied Dr. Hodgson has spoken to him after death. Both of these men were materialists and agnostics, and were brought by Spiritism to believe in God (not in Christianity) and in existence after death in a spirit world.

In addition to this, I may repeat that current opinion in Spiritist circles among the rank and file is, broadly, that the communications with the dead are all genuine (which they certainly are not), and that they are quite easy; whereas Spiritist leaders well know that nothing is more difficult than to get anything authentic.

In a typically successful séance, with a very good medium, six questions were asked, the anwers to which were known (it is believed) to none but the dead; and five were answered.

Mediums cannot know who speaks

May I here, in reference to Professor Hyslop's statement about the trustworthiness of Mrs. Piper, explain this can only refer to her trustworthiness with regard to fraud, for a medium can have no knowledge of thé source of her own communications. Whether they are derived (1) from what her unconscious mind reads from the minds of others, or (2) whether it obtains its knowledge from a discarnate spirit, or (3) whether the information comes from some other inhabitant (not human) of the spirit world, she cannot possibly know. So that her trustworthiness has no bearing whatever on the great question; nor can a medium be called in evidence, save to testify there is no fraud.   This is important.

No doubt other distinguished names, such as Alfred Russel Wallace and Sir A. Conan Doyle, could be added to the above witnesses to belief in necromancy.

Doubters as to Necromancy

Among the doubtful, Professor C. Flammarion says: "That souls survive the destruction of the body I have not the shadow of a doubt. But that they manifest themselves by communications in séances we have no absolute proof."

Some messages received from Professor Hyslop (after his death), through Mrs. Piper, were handed over to Professor Wm. James, to decide whether they were from subconscious sources, or really from Hyslop. He decided that the messages of Hyslop did not furnish any decisive proof whatever of their authenticity. Sir Wm. Barrett advises all those who have attained the assurance of life after death by means of Spiritism *not* to pursue the matter further; but rather to learn more of the spiritual world and spiritual communion from the Christian mystics.

Professor Richet, a Spiritist leader, referring to this question says: "I am not yet convinced."

"Stainton Moses himself," says Myers, "believed the messages came from departed spirits, but there is great doubt whether they did."

J. G. Raupert, in "The Supreme Problem," p. 117, says: "No advance has been made in establishing spirit identity in twenty-five years of study."

Light, a Spiritist magazine, said (March 13th, 1909): "The hardest thing to prove from the other side is identity; and we know of no test that can determine it."

Professor Newbolt considers that, on account of inaccuracies and ignorance, it is doubtful that the communications are from the spirits of the dead.

D. D. Home, in 1855, at Keighley, in Yorkshire, said (speaking of mediums): "The subconscious mentality accounts for much." Coming from the leading medium of his time this is significant.

Maeterlinck and Hodgson

The "Ear of Dionysius," a most complicated classical inferential message, deciphered by the Right Hon. Gerald Balfour, is not very satisfactory evidence of the work of a discarnate spirit, and was not accepted in Spiritist circles without great opposition.

Maeterlinck observes on the subject: "Hodgson

'came back' a week after death. After long talks, Professor James says he felt 'as if an external will was probably there; but could not say it was Hodgson's.' That William James should hesitate to recognise his lifelong friend is most remarkable, for Hodgson's first desire was to establish his own identity. William James asked, 'What have you to tell us about the other life?'

"Hodgson seemed to reply, 'It is not a vague phantasy, but is reality.'

"'Do you live as we do?'

"'Yes, we have houses, but not clothing. No! that's absurd. Wait a moment.' And then another spirit says 'Hodgson has to go out to get his breath (!)'"

"Must we then," says Maeterlinck, "decide that it is thus a departed spirit speaks to us? Not so; the power may all reside in the medium. Our Unknown Guest or Unconscious Mind simulates the dead. It projects sights and sounds, gives premonitions, and establishes psychometry.

Further Difficulties

"In Spiritism there is no fixed doctrine concerning a future life. It varies with the country, and it attributes to various spirits the communications it makes to us. The inarticulate language of the unconscious mind can borrow that of consciousness, and takes on the voice of whatever we believe in."

There is no doubt, as a rule, that the unconscious mind of the medium believes itself to be the voice and spirit of the deceased.

That the presence of one sceptic can paralyse the

"departed spirit" becomes very explicable if the communications come from the unconscious mind of medium and audience. It is, however, inconceivable that the spirit of Napoleon, or Newton, or other great men, can be paralyzed by the presence of an unbeliever at a séance!

If the unconscious mind be denied, we must give up spirit agency once for all, for in a trance the one depends on the other in any case.

"The mind of man is one, but is dual in nature," conscious and unconscious (or objective and subjective, as Hudson calls it). The unconscious mind is constantly controlled by suggested thoughts, and is in easy telepathic connection with both the conscious and unconscious minds of others.

Difficulty of Identification

Professor H. P. Jacks, LL.D., on June 28th, 1917, in his Presidential Address to the S.P.R., raised some important points with regard to the truth of communications from one's departed friends. He pointed out the main problem of Modern Spiritism is the difficulty of identification. He also says: "To prove identity . . . you want as much resemblance as possible" (to the one you knew). "But what greater difference . . . could be conceived than that between an embodied and a disembodied being? No two beings that I can think of could be more unlike one another than myself in my body and myself outside my body.

"What it may be to see without eyes, to speak without a tongue, to move without limbs, I find myself wholly unable to conceive. The difference is so great that I cannot recognise myself under these conditions as the same person I now am.

"We are apt to thrust this difference aside by saying that the true self of a man consists of his moral characteristics. That I do not question as an abstract proposition. But moral characteristics are elusive and difficult to define. I imagine a man would have some difficulty in picking out his wife in a crowd . . . if he had nothing but her moral characteristics to go by. Speaking for myself, I am by no means sure what my moral characteristics are. I would much rather be asked for my weight or my height." Professor Jacks also notes that "there is no proof whatever in Spiritism that the voice comes from 'the other side,' or from spirits, or that these are disembodied. They may come from this world, and other sources altogether."

Some Discrepancies

Another significant point he notes is that those who communicate always retain the distinction of sex. "Must," Professor Jacks further asks, "they always speak in the language of the present day, and not that of the age they lived in; in English or in French? Moreover, they are in *time*, not *eternity*, for they speak of the 'future.' They are constantly getting tired" (which, however intelligible in the medium is inexplicable in them). "They can hear and see! We are led to conclude these are human beings, but this need not prove they are the dead. You cannot separate the individual from his world; and these individuals evidently carry their world with them; for it is ours!"

The point of identity is a most difficult one, in the light of experience. A moment's consideration of the Titchborne case will show this. Here is an impostor recognized as her son, by many infallible signs, by his own mother. A fraud who passed no end of tests, and narrowly escaped being accepted as genuine. As a spirit he would have, undoubtedly, succeeded in proving a false identity.

Some Absurdities

Another point is, that communications come with equal facility from (1) the *genuine* dead, whether they died yesterday or 1,000 years ago (and they all talk precisely the same English); (2) from the *supposed* dead, who have never "passed over," but are still alive and possibly attending the séance; (3) from *imaginary* dead, who have never existed at all (I have instances of long and touching communications from such through reputable media). Moreover, these Spirits are pious with the pious, loving with lovers, business-like with business men, gross and vulgar with the wicked. In England they are sceptical and reasoning; in Germany (*ante-bellum*) mystical; in France frivolous and libertine; in America positive and dogmatic, in Italy atheists and pantheists; in Utah Mormons, teaching that wilful abortion is lawful; in Russia orthodox or nihilist; in Spain freemasons (see "Spiritism Unveiled," Lanslots, p. 107). Such vagaries do more to destroy faith in necromancy than any so-called tests establish it.

Andrew Lang (1911) says "I don't believe in professional mediums, nor that Mrs. Piper com-

municates with the dead as she professes to do."
In Mrs. Piper's case, especially, the statements all
proceeding from the "control," the dead Marseilles,
Dr. Phinuit, are as full and accurate about the living
(whom he could never have known) as about the
dead.

Necromancy a Fallacy

We began with believers and their affirmations;
we will end with denials.

Professor Flournoy, a leader in psychology, takes
the standpoint that beliefs in communications with
the spirits of the dead is a fallacy, but that the facts
are real; and so also is telepathy, clairvoyance, etc.,
though not yet officially recognised by science.

In Spiritism, says a scientist, no absolute message
has come from the dead.

M. Maeterlinck, in "Our Eternity," says: "Why
do departed spirits come back with empty hands and
words? Beyond our last hour (on earth) is it all
bare, and shapeless, and dim?" ("Only," we
might reply, "to unbelievers. To faith all is far
brighter beyond the tomb than on earth. There is
no vague guessing or surmising. The language is
that of certainty: 'We *know* that if our earthly
house, etc.'").

"If it be so," continues Maeterlinck, "let them
tell us (but they don't) of what use is it to die if
all life's trivialities continue? Can we only remember
that we had a great-uncle called Peter, and that our
cousin Paul had varicose veins? They tell us enough
to show they could disclose similar details about the
unknown mysteries.

Cross-Correspondence

"In cross-correspondence (that last and intricate attempt to prove necromancy) a single spirit manifests itself almost simultaneously through several mediums at great distances from each other." Each message by itself is usually unintelligible (being some isolated word, or half a sentence, or an obscure reference that cannot be completed, or deciphered without the remainder).

As Sir Oliver Lodge says, "the object of this complicated effort is to prove that there is some definite intelligence underlying the phenomena." (See Sir Oliver Lodge, "Survival of Man," p. 825). Maeterlinck proceeds: "It is very strange that the 'dead' should bring to us nothing but a kind of ingenious child's puzzle.

"The smallest astronomical or biological revelation would form a far more decisive argument than these literary reminiscences.

Stainton Moses Fails

"Why do they speak so seldom of the future? Even with Stainton Moses there is the same inability to bring us the veriest particle of truth of which no vestige exists on this earth.

"This medium, however, in touch with Grocyn, a friend of Erasmus (of whom few had heard), gave particulars about him which were at first thought new, but which have since been discovered in quite accessible books.

"But Stainton Moses had never read these books; here then is a mystery, but it is not necessary to have recourse to the dead to solve it." It is not the dead," Maeterlinck adds, "who speak and act in Spiritist séances."

It is obviously quite too soon to give a fixed judgment as to the real source of the medium's communications. It is certainly unknown to herself, when no fraud exists; and in such cases, the audience and medium alike, all act in good faith.

The Three Alternatives

The most unlikely and impossible of the three alternatives at present (quite apart for the moment from any article of Christian faith), both on account of insufficient direct evidence for, and the strength of the direct and indirect evidence against it, is the theory that *the source is the spirits of departed human beings;* in short, that it is "necromancy" under a new name.

The second of the three, *that all communications come from medium and audience*, which is the extended and combined telepathic and psychometric theories, would certainly be adopted generally did they but cover the whole ground without quite undue stretching. But no one, even their warmest advocates, say they do, so at most this can only account for part.

The last of the three, *that messages may come from non-human spirits*, when carefully considered, seems the best and most likely alternative for those phenomena that telepathy in its present extended form will not cover.

Too Soon to Dogmatise

Of course the days are young yet, and every year scientific discovery is advancing. Our knowl-

edge does not stand still one moment in the understanding of the spiritual and the unseen, now that
we are free from the paralysing materialism of
Huxley and the monism of Hæckel.

Still, at present, there remains this third alternative for those cases that telepathy will not cover.
Only we must get rid of the fallacious but still popular
Spiritist theory that the only spirits that populate
the unseen world are those of the departed; for
this blocks the way to what thousands of inquirers,
with myself, believe to be the truth.

This truth, like all truths, does not rest on one
point alone, but, once adopted as a working hypothesis, is found to fit in with countless facts that form
indirect proofs.

Bible True pro tem.

Let us all admit then, at any rate *pro tem.*, that the
Bible is true, that the almost universal belief of all
ages is true, and that the other world is densely
peopled with angels and spirits, good and bad,
and very possibly spirits also of a low order, distinguished as dæmons, not one of whom are the
spirits of the dead.

If these spirits can, through the open door of
the medium's trance, find any means of commu-
nicating with our earth, the Spiritist phenomena fit
in far better with such a theory than with any other.
I have an idea that it is not found so difficult
now as it might have been some years ago to thus
extend our belief in spirits into a truer concept
of their orders and of their non-human
character.

It is natural we should discover that if we will not accept revealed truth, and live by faith in this as one does in lesser matters, the only other path is that of experience.

The Fact of Another World

The first point to establish is the fact of another world, and the second, that it is inhabited by intelligences. These two points Spiritism claims to have established.

But it is not till this has been done that further questions arise. What are these intelligences? Can we identify them with our dead? And then, before the days of tests and telepathy, and when all was accepted as true, came the theory, naturally enough, that all spirits in the other world were those of the dead.

But we have got on since those days, and the more we advance the less certain does it appear to be that Spiritists really are in touch with disembodied spirits; more and more are ordinary communications explained by telepathy, and the freakish, inconsequent, and purposeless and meaningless ones that are left are in all probability from the spirit world, but not, I suggest, from the departed dead.

Anything Better than Nothing

It is not quite easy to understand why Spiritists, who have beloved departed ones, should be so anxious to prove that the unworthy, conventional, and trite or foolish and mystic messages proceed from their dear friends.

I suppose one would rather hear anything than nothing, and it is no pleasure to me to suggest that, so far as we have gone, necromancy is the least probable solution of the phenomena observed.

I have pointed out that the first two steps in Spiritism by no means involve the third. Dr. A. D. Husted, for instance says: "I certainly believe in the continued existence of the soul. My belief is based upon experience and on the study of psychology for fifteen years. I take no part in the phenomena of the Spiritism of to-day, which I regard as fraudulent communications."

Professor Van der Naden says: "From forty years of scientific investigation I am absolutely certain of the continuation of life after death."

I venture to say the stated position of these two scientists is that of any Christian throughout the world and of tens of thousands of others to-day; but it by no means implies communications with the dead.

CHAPTER VII

"POSSESSION" AND ALLIED STATES

A Dark Problem

In this chapter and the next we touch on important subjects of great interest, more or less allied to Spiritism; they cannot therefore well be skipped. This chapter, particularly in speaking on "possession," touches on one of the darkest problems of Spiritism, and one which I must dwell on, so strongly do I fell about it.

Many, who know nothing of these occult subjects, must have been surprised and amused when at some friend's house they passed an idle hour in table-turning, or even in planchette* writing, to see the horrified look on the face of one of the bystanders. They cannot in the least understand the earnest warning that follows not to "dabble in Spiritism," and naturally put down the mentor as some faddist or alarmist obsessed by groundless fears. The whole thing looks so absolutely simple and innocent,

---

* Some may not know that this is a small triangular board mounted on two very short wheeled feet, while the support at the apex is an upright pencil. This is placed on a large sheet of paper, and the hands, joined, are laid flat, quite passively, on the wood. After a short time it may begin to move automatically, and write letters and words, or draw figures.

that the warning is disregarded and nothing happens. It may be twenty years after, when happily married, the same lady who was warned long ago, in an idle hour recalls the long-forgotten planchette, and gets it out of the cupboard and sits down to "try her luck." The board responds, and interest is awakened. The recreation becomes a pursuit, soon raps are heard, and then something *does* happen, and the long-forgotten warning is recalled when it is too late.

Such a case is not imaginary, but is outlined from life.

Timely Warning

I myself, driven by my own certain knowledge, have acted as such a mentor more than once. Only the other day, when dining with one of our best known London vicars, I pointed out some of the dangers (the subject of Chapter X.) of table-turning, etc., and in his sermon next Sunday he touched on them. A lady in the congregation who was beginning to dabble in the occult was struck, and wrote to him for the address of the physician who had spoken. The vicar asked my leave to give it, and the lady then wrote to me. I replied and advised her strongly at once to give up all such practices, and soon got a letter back to say she had done so, and was most grateful for the timely warning.

I do not find such renunciations too common, and should recommend any friendly reader, if these warnings do not succeed, to get their friend to read the tenth chapter of this book, or Hugh Benson's "Necromancers." Raupert, a well-known writer, points out that "Planchette and automatic writing may become a source of most disastrous development."

Letters from "Julia"

I quite agree that automatic writing is not in the least reliable as proving any spirit communication. Those who use it may have mediumistic powers, and all the writing may come unknown to themselves, from their own unconscious minds. I do not, myself, doubt that the notorious letters of "Julia" in "After Death" were thus produced; bearing as they do throughout the unmistakable impress of the mind of Mr. W. T. Stead, whose hand unconsciously wrote them. On the other hand, some are objective, and not written by oneself at all.

Many Christian people in such cases, who are quite orthodox, indulge in a pursuit believed to be harmless; but psychic consequences, more or less dangerous, soon follow. The judgment becomes paralysed, the will surrendered, and insanity or "possession" may eventually ensue.

Sir Oliver Lodge on "Possession"

"We really know nothing about the connection between mind and body, the spiritual and the material. We know that each organism belongs to the special psychic character (or personality) that employs it, just as a violin belongs to a special operator, who might resent any other person attempting to play upon it. But that proves nothing as to the impossibility of so utilising it. If it be possible for the normal operator to leave his mechanism open to a visitor, it is a definite fact we may as well know.

"As to the power of dislocation of the usual connection between mind and body, it is supposed to occur (generally) during sleep."[*]

I will now proceed to give, with brevity, a few cases of "possession" known to myself.

What "Possession" is

Perhaps before doing so it may be well, for the benefit of those to whom the whole subject is new to remark that "possession" means exactly what is hinted at by Sir Oliver Lodge; only the "visitor" suggested is always some more or less evil (not disembodied) spirit from another world. It is this that distinguishes "possession" from "double personality," of which we shall speak later. This latter term is best reserved for those cases when the "visitor" appears to be absolutely human, and generally one's own self at another period of life.

"Possession" by an evil spirit is tacitly recognised by most of our alienists. There is no large asylum that does not contain one or more of such cases. These people are often otherwise sane, but are constantly liable to have their bodies used, against their will, by some alien and evil force.

"Possession" in the Holborn Restaurant

The other day a mental physician called on me and asked if I would come and see a well-marked case of "possession." I begged to be excused, for I had seen so many.

* Sir Oliver Lodge, "Survival of Man," p. 172.

"Oh, but you must see this one; it is so remarkable. The man is quite able to go about, and has come over to London to be cured.

"I cannot spare the time."

"Well, come to the Holborn Restaurant and dine with us there."

The Arab Gentleman

He was so earnest about it that I consented, and found myself a few nights later sitting with the doctor opposite to an Arab gentleman, evidently of high breeding. He briefly explained his distressing case. He was of the highest rank in Arabia, but had moved for some years to India, and, being very well off, soon got mixed up with some of the idle rich who dabbled in Spiritism. He commenced with table-turning and planchette writing, but soon began to hear "raps." These pursued him to his bedroom, and his sleep became disturbed with the noises and trying to decipher them. Then he heard voices at the window, and at last one day, he told me with deep earnestness, he heard suddenly the same voice from within; and from then he has lived a life of torment. He was deeply convinced of the evil nature of this "unknown (and unwelcome) guest," for it was ever speaking to him the most impure thoughts in the purest Arabic (not Hindustanee, though it entered him in India), and suggesting horrible crimes and debaucheries.* He said he was only now partially master of himself, and he could no longer drag on such a life, but must

* He particularly pointed out it was a dialect only spoken by the highest classes in Arabia.

commit suicide if he could not be cured. Half-way through the dinner this spirit began speaking, but of course I could not understand a word till the man translated it,—a very weird performance.

A German Lady

Another was a very different case, and was well known to my principal London publisher at the time, and to a lifelong friend, daughter of an eminent Harley Street physician. This was a Christian lady of rank in Germany (*ante bellum*), who, how I know not, became "possessed" of an evil spirit. For nearly two years, at intervals, when sitting at table with friends, or receiving them in her drawing-room, she would suddenly begin to talk in a rough, hoarse, man's voice, saying all sorts of things that purported to be revelations of Satanic mysteries, blaspheming against God, and uttering all sorts of obscenities.* It particularly spoke, with approval, of some supposed miraculous gifts then overrunning Germany, and declared they were sent by the higher evil powers for purposes of deception. After half an hour or so her natural voice would return, and she would resume her conversation where she left off, and was quite unconscious of anything that had happened. Of course her friends declared her mad, and distinguished alienists came to examine her, and found her sane, but "possessed." Great prayer was made for her in large private prayer circles, and in the church, and suddenly one day, after a long and terrible display of evil, the spirit left her, and she was completely restored to her usual

* It is curious how obscenity and profanity go together.

health. This woman was fortunately of exceptional ability; had she had any natural flaw in her mentality, such a visitation would probably be but the prelude to real insanity.

A Lady in Bayswater

Some years ago I had a case that much distressed me. There were two quiet maiden ladies, Christians of the Church of England, living in a small house of their own in Bayswater, and full of good works.

How, I know not, the younger of them was suddenly "possessed" with an evil spirit. The first attack was truly terrible. I was hastily called to the terrace, where they lived, and in the bedroom I found the younger one on the bed, and the elder, staring in agony at her sister, standing at the foot.

The former was simply pouring out blasphemies and obscenities with an ease and rapidity that bespoke long practice. The language used and the animus displayed against God were as remarkable as they were horrible. She was quite unconscious. Her sister, weeping at the foot of the bed, kept declaring that, to her certain knowledge, her sister had never even heard the fearful words she was using so volubly. They had never been in the East End, or visited among the poor, and had led sheltered lives, where no such language was ever heard. It was quite clear to me that the true diagnosis of the case was "possession." After a while, and after violent convulsions, the spirit left her, and quite unconscious of all that had happened, she was her own sweet self again. These scenes were frequently repeated; again most earnest prayer was made, and, without insisting here on direct cause and effect, I am glad to say the "possession" gradually ceased. These true incidents and others that will follow may, I fear, somewhat try the patience of some of my more sceptical readers.

Current Scepticism

Many have indeed read, at any rate in their childhood, that in Palestine in the days of Christ, a long time ago, certain unfortunate people were "possessed with devils." But these were in the Bible, and no such things were to be found in modern life. Not only so, but science had long since professed to discover that even in those times there were not any such "possessions"; that it was simply a case of wrong diagnosis, and that the real character of such a disease had been discovered. All sorts of things at that time were ascribed to spirit agencies in a country where the "evil eye" then was, and still is, a cherished delusion.

"Possession" is a Fact To-day

It must come, therefore, with something of a shock to a thoughtful reader to find a physician and a psychologist risking his reputation (like Sir Wm. Crookes, *longo intervallo*) by speaking of "possession" in the twentieth century. I feel sure that such a reader will soon decide that his own doctor, a sensible man, must see this book at once, which he is quite sure he would not endorse.

Perhaps he would not, unless he were an alienist of considerable experience; but the fact of "pos-

session" is at least as well established as any other
fact in Spiritism, and is, I fear, true.

Bear then a little longer with a very brief sketch
of these horrors. It may be worth your while to do
so, if it leads to any practical result; and is accepted
as a warning, not to be disregarded, against tampering in any way with the powers of the other
world, or indulging in any practices clearly condemned in Holy Scripture; in the truth of whose
words, I cherish a hope, our "thinkers" may yet
be led again to believe. Thank God, there are many,
and these not of least repute, who do so to-day.

The Pious Quaker

A pious Quaker gentleman, a lay preacher, and a
greatly honoured character, was sent me by some
Irish doctors, who could not diagnose the malady.
I considered the case one of "possession." The
attacks I found to be so extremely violent as well as
so noisy physically, and so distressing mentally, that
I had to take a quiet house at Henley-on-Thames and
engage two strong male mental nurses to look after
him, a young residential doctor being in attendance,
while I visited the case as often as I could.

I shall never forget those visits. I seemed to be
standing at the mouth of hell. The grinding of the
teeth, till eventually all of his fine set (not artificial)
were broken into bits and scattered over the room,
the horrible expression of his face, but, above all
the scorching and devilish language, can only be
alluded to. The result was that both male nurses
(as stoical a race as can be found) gave me notice,
saying "that no salary would induce them to

continue to hear such utterances," inured as they both were to the vilest language.

Between the times of the attacks nothing could be gentler and quieter than this aged Quaker.

Real Devil "Possession"

It will be observed that, while I cannot connect these two cases directly with Spiritism, I adduce them in proof of the fact, in the present day, of real "devil possession." This of course, if proved, turns the whole position of those Spiritists who declare the next world is denizened only by the dis-embodied spirits of the dead; for I trust none of my readers will allow that humanity, embodied or disembodied, could ever descend to such depths as I have described.

Professor William James writes: "The refusal of modern enlightenment to treat "possession" as a possible hypothesis. has always seemed to me a curious example of the power of fashion."

Personalities

I now turn to a much less unpleasant subject, that of double, multiple, and alternating per-sonalities.

In these cases two or more personalities (egos) seem to dwell in the same body, sometimes simul-taneously (double and multiple personality), and sometimes in succession (alternating personalities).

I do not call them cases of "possession," inas-much as nothing evil is manifest. Mediums (through the power of their controls?), I believe, unconsciously often seem to have the personality of the speaking "spirit" transferred to them, even to the facial expression, voice, etc. Curiously enough, two of the well-marked cases of alternating personality known to me are both those of Baptist ministers. One was a man, the Rev. Ansel Bourne, who was lost, suddenly disappearing from his town and chapel for two months. The case was investigated by the S.P.R., who found that he was seized with the belief that he was a merchant of the name of A. J. Brown. I never heard whether he had ever known such a man, or if such a man ever existed. Suffice it to say that when he disappeared he bought a shop in another town, stocked it with small wares, and carried it on successfully for six weeks. The name was painted over the door. When found, and brought back, he remembered nothing. R. Hodgson, LL.D., personally examined the evidence and found it absolutely true.

The Infant Minister

A second case was brought to my notice by Dr. Lloyd Tuckey, a well-known London specialist, of another Baptist minister.

Driving home one day, this unfortunate man was thrown out of his gig on to his head. Being delicate such an accident was very serious, but those who brought him home and the doctor who examined him at the time could discover nothing more than that the minister was naturally stunned and dazed. He was carefully undressed and, after some liquid food, was placed in bed. He was a bachelor and lived alone with two servants.

In the morning the housemaid knocked at his

door, but could get no reply. A little later she knocked again, without getting any response. She then turned the handle and opened the door, and saw the Baptist minister lying awake in bed and smiling. Something new and strange in his face alarmed her, and she went out, closing the door, and told the cook. The latter was an experienced married woman and used to emergencies, and declared she would soon find out what it was; so the two returned and entered the bedroom. The Baptist minister still retained his fixed smile, but did not attempt to answer any of the queries as to how he felt, if there was any pain, what he was smiling at, etc.

The Cook's Diagnosis

The cook, evidently a close observer, then noticed a little fluid trickling from the corner of his mouth, and when she smiled at him he began making a low noise, described, I believe, by the initiated as "gurgling."

"Bless his dear heart," cried the cook, in an uneasy ecstasy, "Why, he's a baby; look at him dribbling. Anyhow we will soon see."

A little tea and bread and butter had already been brought in, but nothing would induce the infant-minister to look at them.

The cook went out, and returned with a spoon and some sweetened milk in a saucer. She extemporised a bit and began feeding him in bed. He waved his arms about and kicked his legs in ecstasy, and smiled still more as he took spoonful after spoonful.

Cook, however, delighted with her new charge,

was not content with this, but tried to get nearer to a baby's natural food; and, having brought up several "by hand," got a feeding bottle from home, bought a new nipple for it, and made up the correct lactic mixture, and was rewarded by its being greedily imbibed by the still unsatisfied Baptist minister.

Perplexing Position

Then, of course, came the trouble; he had to be washed and dressed, and that speedily. I have no account of the ablutions, but the clothes were a puzzle, for the case was new to them. Babies they knew, Baptist ministers they knew, but the combination was too much. They eventually compromised as far as they could, avoiding the ridiculous as much as possible, but the effect was very weird.

The cook and housemaid were soon perplexed as to the next step. Of course, such a terrible occurrence could not be kept private, and yet how to tell it? The case did not seem urgent, for the baby was in perfect health, and showed an angelic disposition as the minister crawled about the floor, cooing and gurgling. It was like a nightmare! At last they decided to call in the deacons. These good men, though they tried to look grave and expressed much sorrow at the accident, could hardly conceal their untimely mirth. After consultation they decided that every effort must be made to induce him to occupy the pulpit the following Sunday, and they relied greatly on accustomed sights and sounds to restore him to what they called "his senses."

The Deacons' Effort

So a cab was called and the keys were fetched, and the adult infant was conveyed into his chapel in the strictest privacy. You can picture how in the cab (with the cook who would not leave "the sweet dear") he was stirred up by one deacon's fingers, who solemnly begged and entreated him to be a man, and to remember who he was. An unchanging smile was his only reply. "Don't be a fool, sir," said the other, "remember to-morrow is the Sabbath, and you've got to preach. Here is the chapel," and he pushed the "baby" to the window, quickly withdrawing it, however, when a man passed by. With some difficulty they climbed with the heavy but still smiling burden into the pulpit, placed the minister's two hands upon the open Bible on the desk, and kept him in a standing position by supporting his feeble knees. The devoted cook seated herself in a pew in front of her charge.

"Now, dear, preach me a nice sermon."

The baby did his best, and cooed as well as smiled.

"He'll start singing if he hears the music," said a deacon, and off he went to the American organ and began to play the Old Hundredth Psalm.

Alas, it was hopeless, and when the happy baby began to dribble over the sacred pages the defeated deacons had to remove their minister and get him home with his nurse as best they could.

Recovery

Much of interest transpired which I cannot recount. Suffice it to say, this condition of infancy in mature life might have continued indefinitely had not the babe one day, in the cook's absence, managed to fall, very bumpily, down the stairs, and at the bottom he rose up—the Baptist minister. Naturally he wished to know why he was there and what had happened, over which it took all the cook's wits to draw a decent veil. He continued quite well for some time, but I am informed he has since had another relapse into his early years. He has not, of course, been told of his curious affection, but probably has some indistinct idea of what has occurred.

Both of these are cases of alternating personalities. I have had none of multiple personalities, but other doctors have. Having nothing to do with mad people, but only with nerve sufferers, such do not as a rule come in my way, but are not very rare in asylums. The classical case of three very distinct personalities in a servant girl is perhaps the one described in the greatest detail. I believe it is found in the *Transactions* of the S.P.R.

The case I next record has been under my observation for over twenty years.

Fourteen and Forty

A friend of mine in a country district had a small house for non-normal children, and this girl, one of the inmates, whom I will call Fanny Smith, heard from her a very great deal about me, and began writing to me very beautiful but puzzling letters. They were beautiful on account of their lofty thoughts and amazing grasp of character, and at the same time puzzling because of their extreme simplicity.

I thought her wonderful for the age I supposed

her to be, which was that of a girl from twelve to fourteen. When, however, after a time I heard more details about her, how she loved dolls and toys and the rocking-horse, and how she was often put in the corner, I lowered the age to eight or ten, feeling, at the same time, how impossible it was to think she could have written these clever letters. Suddenly, after I had received a good many, the news came from herself like a bombshell to say (she would have told me before, but she always felt so ashamed of her condition) that she was the daughter of a clergyman and was now forty years of age. I went down to see her for the first time after corresponding for years.

Practically Two People

I found a quiet woman dressed as a child in a pinafore, but with an old face and set figure. With great simplicity and modesty she put to me one or two questions which absolutely posed me. After a time I realised I had here a most interesting case of double personality. Fanny knew perfectly well she was practically two people, unlike the Baptist ministers. At night she used to have rather terrifying times with dazzling lights and other phenomena, and she would get up in the morning a rather naughty child, whom nothing would satisfy but toys and a rocking-horse. On other occasions she would be a clever, middle-aged woman selling tea in the village for the benefit of the funds of the home. She did not seem to pass abruptly from one state to the other, but more or less gradually, and the grown person always knew of the child state and was ashamed of it, and, I presume, to a certain extent the child, only *vice versâ.*

For some years now the child has wholly disappeared and the personality is now but one, and she is a delightful, quiet, sunny, quaint, and deeply spiritual woman.

Established Facts

It will be noted that two of the three cases I have quoted have been of different ages in the same individual. I have met others, but am unable to refer to them. Instances abound, however, where the second personality (like my first Baptist minister) is a being of different tastes and character from the first. The reader may rest assured that double personality and "possession" are as well established scientifically as telepathy, and only those who know the years of scientific labour that has been needed to prove the latter true in spite of all prejudice and opposition, can understand the force of this statement.

It is well to point out, before leaving the subject, that of the seven cases I have given, in two instances only, that of the Arab gentleman and the last case, was the curious condition known to the conscious mind of the sufferer; in the other five it was not so known, though it might be suspected, and there is no proof of normal consciousness when in the abnormal state, though there is plenty of mental vigour.*

* Let me say that the unconscious mind, which, when I first spoke of it twenty years ago, was bitterly scoffed at, and nowhere accepted in English scientific circles, is now a commonplace.

Psychometry

I have already mentioned "psychometry" (or the measuring of another's mind) as having its part in the medium's equipment. It is absolutely necessary, then, to avoid complete bewilderment to the reader, who is patiently moving with distrustful steps amid so many mysteries, to explain and illustrate each term, as far as I can, as we proceed; and I am not without hope that the necessary variety this introduces may have the happy result of inducing the reader to continue reading to the end.

It is probably contrary to all the received canons of literature for an author thus continually to address his readers; but the unusual nature of his task must be his apology.

Psychometry, a sixth (or seventh) sense, was discovered by Dr. Joseph Rodes Buchanan in 1842, but took a good many years to establish, and to the present day is largely unknown. He describes it as the power of the soul (mind) to measure other souls. Like most fathers, he advances great claims for his child. "It is," he says, "the science of divinity (!) in man, whose faculty of intention, by the art of this divine science, enables geologists to see the world in its formation, physicians to watch the progress of disease. Time has no meaning for the psychometrist; the past and the future are to him open books."

Out of this rhapsody I will, at any rate, prove the last sentence true.

We may speak of a secondary consciousness; but the fact remains, that any state of which the individual himself is not conscious is, to him, unconsciousness.

The Stone from Jericho

I used to see before the war, in my consulting room, a young friend studying at University College for the London M.A. She was exceedingly clever in many ways, and hearing she had the gift of "psychometry," of which I then knew little, I tried her with one or two objects lying on my desk, with surprising results. I had recently returned home from examining Professor Sellin's (the Austrian explorer) wonderful work in laying bare, after a burial of 3,000 years, the Jericho, in the Jordan valley, of the days of Joshua.

Being among the first to arrive, little had then been moved (all is now gone), and lying thickly about in the sand in great numbers outside the city were exceedingly heavy round stones, the size of an orange.

I found that in those primitive days these balls, which exactly fitted the hand, were weapons of offence thrown without a sling, probably with either hand.* Most probably the one I brought home was one thrown in the last great struggle in which the city was taken. I placed it without comment in her hand.

The Past an Open Book

Well may Dr. Buchanan say that to the psychometrist "time has no meaning and the past is an open book"; it is so. Never shall I forget the look of frozen horror all over her face the moment she took the ball in her hand. She would not retain it. "Take it away, take it away," she said, "it

---

* Cf. Judges xx. 16, only these stones were *thrown*, not slung.

9—2

is dreadful. I can't bear it." It took some time to quiet her down, and I asked what was the matter. "Oh," she said, "that was a shock. That is a very wicked stone, and it's very, very old. I hear shouts and cries of battle. It all seems so strange, and old, and wicked. What is it? Do you know?" Of course I knew well, for there are few round stones associated with such scenes as this, which she discovered in a moment.

An Asylum Chaplain

A young clergyman, whom she had never seen, then held up the gold cross pendant from his watch-chain and asked her to take it. She held it to her forehead a moment, and of course I now expected something holy and beautiful. Not a bit of it. "Oh, how horrible! I hear shrieks and yells and all sorts of queer noises. Where am I? What is it?"

I looked with surprise at the young man, who, however, did not seem much astonished. "I was chaplain in a lunatic asylum," he said, "for years, and I suppose that's what she hears."

Such powers, it is obvious, would account for much that happens at séances, especially when I reveal the means by which, unconsciously to the psychometrist, it is done. This was told me in another interview.

Psychometrist in Harley Street

A physician I know in Harley Street has himself remarkable powers in psychometry. One afternoon I sat in his drawing-room, accompanied by a friend of mine, a skilled electrical engineer in Government employ.

I handed the doctor the gold pencil with which I corrected this book, and he put it to his forehead,* closed his eyes and at once began the history of the donor very fairly correctly.

"But how," I asked the engineer, "can he describe the donor by the pencil, for she only touched it for a moment when she took it from the shopman and handed it to me?"

"He doesn't," was the reply, "the pencil is of no value to him. He simply reads your thoughts by telepathy, and his holding the pencil keeps your thoughts concentrated on it." I may say that at this time we were alone, the doctor having been called out of the room. "Now," he continued, "I'll show you something more. I can inhibit his brain action at will. Give him something else, and put up your thumb at any time. So long as it is up, I will stop his brain acting; when you lower it, he will proceed."

Inhibiting the Brain

I should say this friend was introduced to the doctor this afternoon for the first time.

The doctor returned, and I took an old letter out of my pocket and gave it to him.

He at once closed his eyes, held it against his forehead, and began.

I should say the letter was from a wealthy Liver-

---

* The idea being that this was the position of the long-lost central eye (Cyclops), now believed to have been connected with the pineal gland. I rather think the place is represented by the infantile "*anterior fontanelle.*"

pool merchant, asking me to undertake the case of
his son, who was much afflicted with nerves.

All this he was outlining, slowly but surely, fairly
well, when I quietly raised my thumb. "The boy
suffered from — from — I can't see it, its all
muddled."

"Go on," I said.

"I can't," he replied, "it's all blurred; I feel
confused. I was never like this before," and he
opened his eyes.

"Shut your eyes," I said, "it's all right. Try
and go on," and I turned my thumb down.

He at once said "Yes, it's all clear, 'from nervous
debility,'" and he told me all I knew.

A Puzzling Case

I purposely record this, though my friend's action
was not psychometry, because if not collusion and a
trick, which I do not believe it was for a moment,
it indicates there may yet be other powers latent in
some, of which we are not aware.

"Now," said my friend, "ask him a question of
which you do not know the answer yourself."

"Where is my youngest sister, and what is she
doing?"

The doctor had nothing to hold, but closed his
eyes and began:

"I see two ladies seated on a small platform at a
table covered with a cloth—I think it's green" (it
wasn't) "in a wooden building with an iron roof. A
good number of serious-looking people are sitting
before them, to whom one of the ladies, I think your
sister, is speaking."

"I haven't the least idea," I said, "whether you are right. But I'll write and see, and let you know." I found he was.

Further Puzzles

This case has sorely puzzled me. At last I've thought that, after all, at the time I was thinking of my sister, then engaged on a mission, and that so possibly he may have got it partly from my brain.

It was quite clear the doctor had no more idea than the medium (save in theory) of how he obtained his knowledge; so that in the case of a medium, whether her utterances came from a spirit or from her audience's (unconscious) minds through her own telepathic powers in either case, she could not tell.

Substances held in the hands of mediums, and of most with telepathic or psychometric (practically the same) powers, can sometimes be tasted, and may even act medicinally. This is seen, not only with medicines, but with most other substances, in various ways.

CHAPTER VIII

SECOND SIGHT AND APPARITIONS

THE bearing, direct and indirect, of this chapter on the phenomena of Spiritism will be seen to justify its contents. I will begin with my personal experience of "second sight."

Extent of Vibrations

We all know that the spectrum represents the very limited range of our ordinary vision, at any rate as regards colour, and that further ranges of vibrations of what would equally be colour, could we see them, extend on either side.

Sir Wm. Crookes points out that vibrations from 16 to 36,000 per second are known to us as sounds. From 36,000 to 1,000,000,000 (a pretty large range) they are imperceptible. Above 1,000,000,000 they are perceived as electricity. From 2,000,000,000 to 250 billions (!) (a still greater jump) the vibrations are again imperceptible. From 250 billions to 1,000 billions they are again seen as light and colour, from infra-red to ultra-violet. From 1,000 billions to 250,000 billions (!) they are imperceptible for a third amazing gap, while from 250,000 billions to

5 *trillions* (?)* they form the recently discovered "X" rays. It is quite evident that there lies an enormous region of "potential" sight or of other wonders in this as yet "unseen world" of vibration. In time, if we consider the whole range of vibrations per second as extending the space of a year, the extent of those known to us are as one second; that is, as a second is to a year so is the known to the unknown. In space, the known vibrations as compared with the unknown are as less than an inch to a mile! As far as I understand it, true "second sight" that visualises invisible things is often only an abnormally acute physical vision;† at other times it refers to true psychic vision.

Auras

"Auras" constitute another of our recent discoveries, and are the lineal descendants of the time-honoured "haloes," with which early sacred art never failed to adorn the heads of its holy subjects. We now find, to our great surprise, they are facts, and not the imagination of visionaries or the fancies of the mediæval; but alas, at the same time, we also discover that they are neither confined to the head, nor to the holy, for they surround the whole bodies of just and unjust alike.

Many of the ancients, however, in this, as in much else, had something more than an inkling of the truth.

Paracelsus says: "The vital force is not enclosed

* A billion is a million (not a thousand) millions, and a trillion is a million billions, numbers wholly inconceivable. It is equally inconceivable how these facts are ascertained.

† That can take up vibrations beyond the ultra-violet.

in man, but radiates round him like a luminous sphere"!

Dr. Kilner's Work

Dr. Kilner, in the West End of London, has devoted a great deal of his life to the study of auras, concerning which he has learned much, and what he has discovered he turns to valuable use for diagnosis in his daily practice.

Most kindly, finding out my interest in these phenomena, he showed me all he knew, and, what was most important, how a non-sensitive like myself, a man who has no hypnotic or visionary powers, could actually be made to see the aura.

Experts like the physician in Harley Street, whose psychometric powers I considered in the last chapter, can see the aura in colours. This is a purely natural and, as I believe, hereditary gift. One cannot be enabled artificially to see the aura in colours, but any one can see it for himself as a distinct mist or halo.

Before the war, I believe the firm of Baillière, Tindall and Cox, Charing Cross, used to sell a box, complete with all requisites and instructions for seeing the aura.

Seeing the Invisible

I found that what was required to see the invisible was to place the patient in front of a black velvet curtain opposite to, and about ten feet away from, the window. A solution (blue) of dicyanin (a salt, I believe, of some ingredient of opium with cyanic or hydrocyanic acid),* which could not be procured during the war, is then placed between two flat sheets of glass about half an inch apart, so as to form a sort of coloured screen, through which one can look. It is best about six inches long. It is then held up before both eyes in a bright window light, and one looks up through the blue screen for at least five minutes steadily into the sky. The screen is then laid aside, and one finds at once it has produced abnormal acuteness of vision, which lasts an hour or two. Print which previously could not be read without glasses now requires none.

The blind is then drawn down, so as to darken the room, and, with one's back to it, one gazes steadily at the patient standing facing you in front of the black velvet curtain. After a time you see a striated mist all round the body and extending nearly six inches. It does not ascend as if it were heat exhalations, but stands straight out in health, drooping, as seaweed out of water, in ill-health.

Description of Aura

I put my two hands in front of me, and there, streaming from my fingers, was the aura. When the tips of the fingers were ten inches apart their auras touched.

The aura does not become visible for the first half-inch from the body. In a woman it is almost twice the length of a man's aura. It is not any sort of vapour, for it is the same whether the patient be hot or cold, and it never rises. The aura from

* Let no one write letters to me inquiring about this preparation. I can give no further information.

the tips of the fingers can be lengthened, by will power, from five inches to over a foot (as I have seen by actual experiment). From my experience I judge that the rays of the aura (in common possibly with those of the astral body) [ghosts] are a little more rapid than the ultra-violet. It must be remembered that the rays of the aura are not the only ones that are not visible to the material sight. Heat rays of less rapidity than 250 billions per second are all invisible. The hot iron gives them off all the time, but only when it becomes red are the rays rapid enough to be seen as colour. The "X" rays are also quite invisible ordinarily, though they can destroy the skin.

What is it.

There is also evidence that in all ages some men and women have been able to see many of these invisible rays; for the aura is drawn on the walls of ruins in India, Egypt, Peru, and Yucatan. In the South Kensington Museum are figures with the aura shown, of the year 324 B.C.

For want of a better name, one calls the aura an emanation of "nerve force," natural electricity, magnetism, psychic energy and the like. All of these are terms either inaccurate or hopelessly without meaning, and expressions rather of our ignorance than of our knowledge.*

---

* Still acuter vision is said to see "thought forms" with equal clearness, and Leadbeater's interesting book depicts these in colours in great variety. Evidence is slowly accumulating to show that thoughts as they leave us may be seen as definite entities, with shape and colour. As, however, this interesting study is quite outside our subject, it will not be touched on.

Auras in Colour

Auras are seen in over twenty distinct colours by a few and these are found to correspond to the character of the person. My friend in Harley Street sees them very distinctly round every person he meets, all day long.

A dean's widow, who lives in Scotland, is quite as good, and she knows the disposition of people by their aura when they enter the room. Her mother had the same power; and what rather distresses her is, it is developing in her son of six, though she has never mentioned it to him. "I don't like that 'brown' man," he said when a friend left;* and at another time expressed his approval of the "blue" lady! I could write much more on this interesting and little known subject but refrain.

Let the sceptical reader, however, note in passing, that the facts I speak of are well established among students all over the world.

The "N" Rays

These, indeed, are the much discussed "N" rays of Dr. Becquerel, and have been shown to be rays of light a good deal more rapid than those at the violet end of the spectrum, as I have suggested. They vary much in various diseases, and so can be used in diagnosis. This, I think, is the first stage in seeing the invisible, and the only one that can be produced artificially.

When we go on further clairvoyance is entirely a

* I am always seen by this lady in bright yellow; also by the doctor in Harley Street.

natural gift. It is common among all Celts and is called "taish" or second sight. The forty volumes of the S.P.R. and the "Phantasms of the living"* teem with well-authenticated instances.

The next two personal examples of clairvoyance illustrate a remark of Professor Bray's: "We photograph our mental states on all the rooms we inhabit."

Second Sight

A young friend of mine, a curate of a West End church, when dining with me, said he had just come through a remarkable experience. On being appointed to the curacy after leaving Oxford, he took a small newly-decorated house near the church, and retiring to rest on the first night, no one being in the house but the two servants, who were asleep, he knelt down to pray by his bed. His portmanteau stood in a corner of the newly-papered room. Suddenly he became acutely conscious of a presence in the room, and opening his eyes he saw that this portmanteau had disappeared, the new wall-paper had also gone, and there in an old arm-chair sat a very ancient dame, evidently in a tremendous rage. She had a stick in her hand which she shook violently at him, and her mouth moved rapidly, for she was clearly cursing him, though no sound was heard. Knowing no fear, he gazed at her steadily, and saw her slowly disappear; and gradually the dirty old paper behind her was replaced by the new, which had vanished, and his portmanteau reappeared and all was as before. He determined to get to the

* Myers and Gurney.

bottom of this mystery, and next morning went off to the house agents. "Now that I've taken the house on a three years' lease," he said, "you may as well tell me what's wrong with it. Has anything dreadful happened there?"

Old Lady and Prayer

The agent looked confused, and eventually admitted that a baby had been murdered in the bathroom; but that did not help my friend.

He was then firmly assured this was the only event of interest connected with the house.

Going home he met one of his fellow-curates.

"Hullo," said the curate, "where are your diggings?"

"I've taken a house," said my friend, "No 245, Victoria Road."

"245! Why that was on my beat. I know that house well. I've good reason to."

Scenting a story, my friend asked "Why?"

"When I was on that district," was the reply, "in that house lived an old lady of an incredible age. She was always upstairs in her room, and I used to visit her every week. She liked my coming, and talking and reading to her; but if I attempted to pray she got in a dreadful fury, and declared she would not 'be prayed at.' She slways shook her stick at me."

"I saw her last night," said my friend, "when I was praying, and she shook her stick at me."

Impressions on the Ether?

I was so impressed with this first-hand story that I told it to a most expert occultist whom I knew that I could trust, and he said, "that in the present state of scientific knowledge the best way of accounting for these phenomena of second sight was not by supposing them to be spirits of the dead (or their astral bodies), but rather that some permanent impression had been made on the 'ether' of the room, which could always be seen by any with 'second sight,' and it was in this way that 'haunted rooms and houses' could be explained." Of course, all was pure hypothesis, for even the "ether," as I explained elsewhere, has not yet been scientifically proved. I must add that my friend the curate had the gift of "second sight."

At another time I was staying with an old friend, a Lady C——, at her beautiful place in Cumberland, and one day she motored me over to a celebrated show-house, where the Speaker of the House of Commons was in residence that year, but which we were still allowed to see over.

Fighting for 200 Years

Lady C——, tired with the long drive, sat down in the hall while the mistress of the house was summoned. Suddenly, with great agitation, she shouted to me, "Oh, do stop those men! Whatever are they doing? It's dreadful." pointing with a shaking finger to a corner of the large hall. I could see nothing, "What is it?" I said.

"Don't you see them fighting in that corner." she cried, "those two men? That old one is sure to kill the other," she cried. "Oh! do stop them!"

Just then the mistress came, and asked for the

cause of the agitation. When she was told she did not seem at all surprised.

"Oh, yes," she said, "many people see that, but I've never seen it myself. It is a father and son who fought in that corner about 200 years ago, and some who come see them fighting still!"

The Vision of a Monk

We went upstairs into the fine library, with its lovely views all over the Eden valley, and Lady C—— sat down at the end of the table in the Speaker's usual seat. He was away at the time.

"Whatever is that young man doing by the door?" she said to me.

"What young man?" I asked.

"Why, don't you see him in that brown cloak? He looks like a monk, and he keeps putting his hand out to the wall as if he were trying to take books out of it."

"No," I said, "I see nothing." So I went to the lady, who was standing at the other end of the room and told her of the apparition.

"Oh, yes," she said, "that's a young monk who lived here a long time ago. I'll show you his portrait in the next room. People often see him. He's taking books off the shelf. There used to be book-shelves right up to the door where he is standing, but they've long been taken away."

The Gift of Second Sight

Here, then, are interesting cases of clairvoyance personally known to me. I may say that Lady C—— has the gift of "second sight," and is a clever and interesting lady, very practical, and full of good works.

The above are instances of apparitions seen by those possessed of "second sight," and who on many occasions have seen the invisible.

There are, however, many other cases of apparitions that have appeared to ordinary people, who have no such gifts, and who perhaps have had but one such vision in the course of their life.

Apparition to Non-Clairvoyants

The apparition I am about to record impressed me very much, being that of my own brother. The ladies to whom he appeared had never seen a vision before, and had no gift of "second sight," and, so far as I know, never saw an apparition again. They were not in the least frightened, but very sad, at the supposed loss of their sister, who is still alive, though both her sisters have died.

Many years ago my brother, an Oxford scholar and a missionary, died suddenly in inland China from typhus fever, caught from a patient whom the porter had admitted, after being forbidden to do so, into his hospital at Tai-yuen-fu in Shansi.* The night he died he was seen at the foot of the beds of two of his wife's sisters, who were stationed in different parts of India. They wrote to each other about it, and agreed that he must have appeared to tell them of their sister's death, who was in delicate health at the time; never dreaming it was my brother who had been taken away. It is significant that both took the apparition as a

*Now rebuilt as the "Schofield Memorial Hospital."

matter of course, and also that a third sister, my wife, saw no vision at all. None of the three was "clairvoyant."

It was not till many weeks after, by way of England, they learned my brother had died that night, and that their sister was well.

Apparitions Common

Maeterlinck says, "Neo-spiritism or scientific spiritism maintains that the dead do not die entirely. That their spirit and animistic entity (soul) continues an active existence."

The *naïveté* of all this is striking, when what has been the cherished faith of Christendom during the whole of our era should be now announced as a new and somewhat doubtful discovery, and so quoted by a brilliant modern writer.

These apparitions, of which I have given an instance, are very common within one week of the death of the person.

Mrs. Sidgwick received, in answer to an inquiry, 17,000 replies from people who had seen them; and Mr. Gurney, joint author with Mr. Myers of "Phantasms of the Living," 6,000.

Apparitions before Death

After years of investigation the S.P.R. reported that between death and apparitions after death of the same person, or before death apparitions to the dying, there exists a connection *not due to chance*.

Evidence, indeed, seems indisputable that, just before death, a glimpse of loved ones is often given to the dying person. And it is equally certain that

10—2

shortly after death the form of the dead person
(astral body?) appears to relatives and friends at a
distance.

It is stated scientifically, on what authority I
know not, with regard to this, that the production
of genuine apparitions (unconsciously and involuntarily) resembling the person they profess to represent is a possibility within the range of psychic
power; in other words, that it can be projected
subjectively by the seer's own unconscious
mind.   At best this is but a surmise, and we require
to advance a good way before it will be established
as a fact.

Trend of Psychic Advance

Facts, however strange, have to be admitted on
sufficient evidence. How they are produced, and
all questions relating to cause and effect, and the
formation of hypotheses, must be most tentatively
advanced and never used as dogmas. The present
trend of all psychic progress is doubtless to
show that countless facts which we were certain
were objective (*i.e.*, produced by others) are one
and all subjective (*i.e.*, produced unconsciously by
ourselves).

The next case is quite different and raises the
question of the pre-existence of the future. To our
minds it seems, when we consider it, equally difficult
to believe it does not pre-exist as to believe that it
does.

The wife of a clergyman at Folkestone was an
old patient of mine, a member of a well-known
English family, and one gifted with a certain amount

of "second sight." She wrote and asked me a very curious question.

Seeing the Future

"Can you tell me why God allows me to see the future, but in such a way that I cannot help the friends I know? I will give you three instances of what I mean."

Of these I will briefly record two.

"The other day," she wrote, "I saw myself standing by the side of a steep hill I knew well, near Folkestone, and a car full of ladies dashed past me. At the bottom of the hill, on the main road, was a cart going slowly along full of stones, and the motor dashed into it, and the people were thrown out and apparently hurt.

"Now, as they passed me they were all looking the other way, and I could not see their faces.

Useless Foresight

"A fortnight after I saw in the papers that a party of my friends, going down that very hill, had met with the very accident I saw, but could not prevent, because their faces were turned away. Why was this?"

She said that she generally saw things about a fortnight before they happened.

The other case was that of a lady she saw driving in a victoria, but the lady had her parasol over her face, so that my patient could not see it as she drove past her in the vision. Just then a hansom cab drove up and dashed into the carriage, throwing the

lady out, whose face was still invisible, and she broke
her arm.   My friend watched the papers, but no such
incident was recorded anywhere.   She then had to go
to Westgate-on-Sea, and about a week later took
up the *Daily Mail*, and there was the accident to the
wife of the pastor of the City Temple fully described,
exactly as seen three weeks before, and the result—
a broken arm.   But this unfortunate lady was one
of my patient's dearest friends.   "Why, then," she
asks, "did she have her parasol over her face so
that I could not see and warn her?"

Visions of Future Common

It is quite evident from innumerable instances,
very many from the Highlands, that future events
are often seen before they happen, but in a truly
perplexing way; for it seems to do no good.   If it
did, and any accident were averted, then the vision
would be false, for it would show what, after all,
never occurred.   I don't pursue the perplexing subject,
as I am writing on "Spiritism" and not on "Second
Sight."

I merely give these instances that we may better
understand that we are surrounded with mysteries,
and that many of us possess special faculties, which,
developed as they doubtless are in mediums, may
go far to explain much that puzzles us in séances,
and which we at present believe, perhaps erroneously,
to be the work of "spirits."

Turning from "second sight," I will now give a
remarkable and perplexing instance of clair-audience,
a kindred faculty to clairvoyance.

Clairaudience

Professor Hyslop tells us of a woman who felt something vague was going to happen that she dreaded. Then after a month, when she was sitting sewing at a garment for her child, she heard a voice saying, "She'll never need it." Then a week before the child died the mother thought there was a smell of fire and got very careful that matches should not be left about. Then, only one hour before the fatal event, she suddenly determines to destroy all the nursery matches.

"She takes the child up to its cot for its morning sleep, and once more hears the voice, 'Turn the mattress.' She says she will, as soon as the child has had its nap. So she goes down the stairs and soon after hears a cry.

"She rushes up, finds the child on fire, and it dies in her arms.

"Just too little information to make it effective! And yet this story is only one out of a hundred such. The solution is equally difficult, whether we regard the messages as from one's own unconscious mind, or from departed spirits, or from other spirit agencies.

What is the Use?

"Of whom is sport being made? Is the future unavoidable? If so, why speak of it at all?

"Either they truly foretell an event with some fatal omission, which makes the telling of it useless, or they give details, and we avail ourselves of the warning, and show they did *not* truly foretell the future."

No doubt the problem is not really so insoluble as it appears at first sight. Still, the whole matter is deeply mysterious, and will, I think, reward continued patient investigation.

I will now close with one or two illustrations of warnings that were not futile, and I think, if the whole subject could be tabulated, it would be found that, after all, the number of warnings that saved life or health are more numerous than those of Professor Hyslop's class, just narrated.

Useful Warnings

Maeterlinck tells us of Jean Dupré, the sculptor, who was driving with his wife, when suddenly on the edge of a cliff they heard a voice, "Stop!" They turned and saw no one, but the cry was repeated, and at last the sculptor saw the left wheel of the gig had lost its linch-pin and was on the point of leaving the axle, when they would have gone over the precipice."

Was this voice subjective or objective? Personally I can testify that there are times when it is impossible to decide this question which looks so simple. I have heard a voice call me and speak as clearly as if it were objective, and have asked the friend with me if he had called out, and found he had said and heard nothing, and the voice was from my own mind, and in this case had no meaning. I thought carefully over this instance, and came to the conclusion that the imaginary voice was not like an idea, but had the full sound of a real, strong voice. I am firmly of opinion that imaginary sights and sounds of what isn't to be seen or heard are often perfectly indistinguishable from real objective vision and hearing. The two are identical.

To What are They Due?

Maeterlinck also inquires, "Are these warnings due to subliminal consciousness or are they spirit warnings?" We cannot always tell.

One can, of course, only judge by the facts in each case. In the case of Dupré the warning was clearly providential, and one must judge that it was objective, in common with other visions. Joan of Arc, with her well-authenticated "voices," that altered the destiny of France, is a widely known example.

Irresistible Impulse

"Although," says Maeterlinck (I think too sweepingly), "these premonitions are generally futile, they are not always so. A traveller approaches an unknown town in the dark, and suddenly feels an irresistible impulse (on the road) to turn (his horse); he obeys, and next day discovers had he gone a few feet further on, he would have slipped into the river, and probably been drowned.

"A traveller in South America descends a river in a canoe; the party are just about to sail round a promontory, when a mysterious voice orders them at once to cross to the other side of the river; this appears so absurd that he has to threaten the Indians with death, to force them to do it; but they have scarcely got half-way across when the promontory falls at the very spot where they meant to round it."

Dr. Hodgson, the protector of Mrs. Piper in America, the Spiritist we have so often spoken of, tells us of a dentist bending over a bench where he was vulcanising some rubber with copper, and hearing a voice saying, "Run to the window, quick!" he ran to the window, when suddenly there was a tremendous report, and, looking round, he saw that the copper had exploded, destroying all that part of the work-room.

Many in Great War

I will not repeat thrilling stories of similar occurrences in the Great War, such as that of the "Angels at Mons" and many others, as I feel I have said enough fully to present the subject of sights and sounds that do not exist, though seen and heard, both by those with "second sight," and by ordinary people—some proving futile, others of the greatest value. It will be noted, however, that in every instance that is of value the future is not shown, so that the action taken does not invalidate the picture or message given.

I confess the whole subject is still enshrouded in the deepest mystery. Fortunately, my object here is not so much to account for the phenomena as to establish the facts.

CHAPTER IX

COLLECTIVE HYPNOSIS

The Brass Plate

HALLUCINATIONS are one of the commonest forms of self-deception, and are often extremely difficult to explain or to account for. A cousin of mine, a fleet surgeon in the navy all through the war, and now working for the Admiralty, called last June, and in course of conversation told me that a great friend of mine, a Scotch physician who lived near, had just taken Sir Victor Horsley's old house in Cavendish Square. I was much surprised, and said I had only seen him in Harley Street that day, and had heard nothing of it, and I asked him how he knew.

"Well," he said, "I was coming to you and crossed through the Square, and saw a brass plate on Sir Victor's old house, and out of curiosity I went up and read it, and there was your friend's name on his door-plate."

When he had gone away I went to see if it were true. I found the house on the side of the Square next to Oxford Street. The door and whole building were dilapidated, and no sign of a brass plate anywhere. I met the Scotch doctor, who said he had no intention of moving from Harley Street, and never had. One month afterwards my grandson in the artillery, and stationed at Winchester, came up to town, a rare event for him. He knew nothing of what I have narrated, and came direct from the station to me; nor did he know of my doctor friend.

Daylight Hallucination

We had a long chat, and then, thinking it would interest him, I told him of my cousin's statement, and that I had found it was not true. "What name did he see?" he asked. "Dr. Blair Campbell," I replied.

"Well," he said, "it's very curious, but you are wrong. I've just come through the Square, and reading the plates as I passed, there was the name of Dr. Blair Campbell as large as life." "Where?" I said, greatly mystified. "On the far side of Cavendish Square, next Oxford Street. It was on the right-hand side of the door, on a small brass plate, and there was no other name."

"Well," I said, "that man is a friend of mine, and I must see what all this means, for I'm sure there is no such name there."

We went out together. He was absolutely confident, and said he was prepared to make an affidavit before any judge that the plate was there. However, though we inspected every door, there was no such plate, and Sir Victor's house was still untouched since his death in Mesopotamia.

No Solution

So far I have received no solution of this hallucination. It is only one of an innumerable series, and shows how fallacious our ordinary vision may be.

Pepper's ghost, and the marvels of a sheet of clean glass on a darkened stage, gave some a nasty shock at the time as to the reliability of their senses; but here in broad daylight, by some unknown agency, the same hallucination absolutely deceives two men in perfect health at different times.*

Séance Conditions

When we consider the darkened room, the droning hymns, the tightly grasped hands, the eager expectation, the intense desire to see something, that possesses all alike, and the predisposition of the class of people most frequently found in Spiritist circles, one begins to wonder, and I suggest, not after all without reason, whether the apparitions and materialisations seen in the dim light, and believed in with the utmost certainty, may not in some cases, in a manner, I quite own, as yet imperfectly understood, prove to be some form of hallucination?

After all it is much easier to believe that such may be the case, in such favourable conditions, than that the same hallucination was possible to two separate individuals in the heart of London, at different times, in the open air and bright light of a summer morning.

But there is more than this, as will be seen, in the title of this chapter.

Power in Crowds

There is the power of crowds. Once these can be pervaded by a common thought, or a common object, they tend to fuse, to lose their individuality,

* The S.P.R. are kindly investigating this case.

and to become more or less as one gigantic personality, of great danger for evil, or of great power for
good. Such a condition can be produced by a
powerful orator (by what is called "magnetic
power") in full daylight, and in the open air; by
a less powerful one in a tent. The condition really
becomes hypnotic, reason is in abeyance, and whatever is presented to the collective mind seems
objective to the senses, and thus sights are seen,
and sounds are heard (hallucinations, as in the rope
trick), that are merely the projection, objectively,
of ideas that obsess the mind when in this condition,
which may fairly be called "collective hypnotism."
Semi-darkness, crooned hymns, absolute contact
between every member of the crowd, stillness, and
a powerful common interest seldom fail in producing this condition, as we shall see. I will proceed
later on to record the most remarkable illustration
of this somewhat rare state that it has been my lot
to see.

Collective Hypnotism

Collective hypnotism is a subject but little known,
and was first explained to me by Dr. Milne Bramwell
some years ago. At that time he was practising in
Wimpole Street and seeing large numbers of patients
requiring hypnotic treatment daily. For the benefit
of the uninitiated I may explain that the modern
treatment does not in the least depend on inducing
artificial sleep, nor is it connected in the smallest
degree with the spirit world or the occult. On the
contrary, it may be claimed that the *modus operandi*
is based on the laws of nature and is now fairly well

known, since the discovery of the un- or sub-conscious mind. The whole procedure tends to impress deeply on the patient's subliminal (Myers) mind, beneficial suggestions. calculated to restore the patient to health. So far there does not seem to be much connection between this science and Spiritism. But "collective hypnotism," at any rate, has a very close connection indeed with Spiritist séances, as I shall proceed to demonstrate, and may possibly be a key to much more.

Dr. Bramwell's Demonstration

My only regret is that I was not myself present when the following demonstration took place, but I can vouch for the substantial accuracy of the record. It must be premised that by "Collective hypno-tism" I mean the sub-conscious power that persuades crowds assembled for some common purpose to believe they saw what was suggested to them, but which was really not to be seen; or that they heard what was not to be heard, if suggested to them at the time; but to come to my record.

Dr. Bramwell was busy with his patients one morning when a doctor friend called in, who was much interested in hypnotism. Dr. Bramwell told him that if he would like to see an exhibition of "collective hypnotism," as his waiting room was full of patients in a favourable condition for the experiment, he would probably be able greatly to interest him.

The Turk on the Table

The visitor, naturally, was only too glad of the rare opportunity, and as the two doctors entered the waiting room all the patients looked up. "Ha," exclaimed Dr. Bramwell, "whoever is that sitting cross-legged on the table?" and pointing to nothing with great earnestness and excitement. "Why, I declare it's a Turk with his scarlet fez, smoking a long pipe." "Look, doctor! Look!" he almost shouted. "He is rising! Can you see? Look under him. You can now see the light between him and the table!" The visitor bent his head to look, and several of the patients did the same.

"Now, now," he called out excitedly, "his head almost touches the ceiling! There, he has touched it! He can't get any higher! Yes, he can! There! his head is going through the ceiling! Look, doctor!" he shouted. The visitor stared up, and so did every one in the room, as Dr. Bramwell graphically described the Turk slowly and gradually disappearing through the ceiling, till at last his feet were gone. "He's vanished!" said Dr. Bramwell. "Come along;" and he took the visitor back into his consulting room.

The Danger

"Now," he said, "I want you to understand the importance of what you have just witnessed. All in that room are perfectly certain they have seen a Turk sitting, smoking, cross-legged, on my dining table, and then slowly rise and disappear through the ceiling; and what is more, one and all would on their oath testify to the supposed fact before any magistrate in perfect good faith."

In this way things may be truthfully sworn to that never occurred, and thus the condition may easily produce situations of great danger and induce many beliefs in fictitious phenomena. There is little doubt that the condition tends to prevail, more or less, in large crowds in proportion as they are of one heart and mind. The testimony of thousands in India has been given to a phenomenon that never occurred. These have asserted they have seen a boy throw the end of a long rope up into the air, where it became rigid, and climb up it and disappear, being afterwards found in the crowd.

Séance in Regent's Park

Perhaps one of the most remarkable displays of the power of "collective hypnotism" occurred at a séance at which I was present, and can therefore vouch for the truth of the smallest details. It was not long before Mr. Stead's death that I heard that most wonderful manifestations had taken place at his house at Wimbledon before himself and, I believe, Sir Oliver Lodge and others, where a materialisation of a spirit took place, and he saw standing in the room before him a dear member of his family, who had died shortly before. Of the fact he appeared to have no doubt whatever; and the event made such a deep impression upon him, that with such wonderful mediums as the man and his wife (*from America*) who had operated, he though it a favourable opportunity to restore the (at that time) somewhat fading belief in Spiritism* by producing in London, before a distinguished audience, phenomena wholly supernatural that could not be gainsaid.

* This was before "Raymond," or Sir A. Conan Doyle.

I Attend Officially

I may say I had known Mr. Stead for many years, through evil and good report, and was not therefore in the least surprised to see him one day at Harley Street. He told me of this forthcoming effort, of the wonderful demonstration at his own house, and said he now required the services of four physicians from Harley Street on the following Friday to carefully and privately examine the two mediums, and thus effectively guard against fraud.

I had to read a paper on the following Monday at the Philosophic Institute on "The Borderland"; and hoping I might learn something of value, though I refused at first, I consented eventually to attend and examine one of the mediums in private, with another physician. On the Friday I met the other doctor at a large house in the neighborhood, and soon the mediums arrived. The man was met at the front door, taken by two doctors into the pantry, stripped and examined, and then dressed in an old suit of the footman's and kept isolated in the room. The woman was taken to the top of the house, carefully examined at her own request for any concealed apparatus, etc., and re-dressed in a skirt, blouse, stockings and shoes *only*, and kept alone in the bedroom. She never saw her husband till after the séance.

Remarkable Audience

In the large drawing-room a "cabinet" in the corner was prepared by two screens with a broad space between, over which a pole and curtains were fixed, and inside the only thing was a chair from the kitchen. The company was by invitation only, and was large and distinguished, including men and women of the highest rank, the greatest experts, psychologists from Oxford and Cambridge, intelligent men and women known all over the world,* all earnest inquirers after "truth." One and all were satisfied that there was no opening for fraud or trickery, neither the mediums nor audience having ever been in the house before.

The woman then entered the room between two doctors, of whom I was one, and was placed in the "cabinet" behind the curtains, on the chair. The husband was then brought in and seated amidst the crowded audience. Mr. Stead had a chair near the screen, while I sat facing the entrance to the "cabinet" through the curtains, and looked round on the eager circles of well-known faces with interest. We were then directed to join hands, and did so; but this was not enough, so we took off our gloves, and our bare hands were clasped together for over two hours.† To increase the (hypnotic) effect the room was darkened, and in the gloom American revival hymns were crooned, somewhat discordantly ("Shall we meet beyond the river," etc., etc.), by grave and distinguished men of science! A hoarse voice then shouted from the "cabinet" (the woman) that "the colonel" said the conditions were not yet right.

* I am only sorry I cannot give the names of those present, when it would be seen that the events I shall narrate must be absolutely incredible, unless such an audience were under some unknown force, such as "collective hypnotism."

† Nothing tends so to produce one common thought and feeling, as to form a circle and establish contact by clasping each other's bare hands.

The First Sensation

At this stage *the first* dramatic sensation of the afternoon occurred, and to this I beg close attention. The husband (in the footman's suit) suddenly rose from among the audience, and said, with a strong American twang, "Before our séance begins, ladies and gentlemen, I should like you all to understand that we are NOT mediums, *we are professional entertainers*. We make no claim whatever to powers from the spirit world, of which we know nothing. But we shall produce such phenomena here this afternoon that I hereby offer the sum of one hundred pounds to any London hospital to any one who can produce the same phenomena under the same conditions."

One would have thought that the dropping of such a bombshell in such an audience would have broken up the séance in confusion and indignation. Not a bit of it. The hymns, the close and darkened room, the tightly clasped hands, had already done their work and produced a certain amount of collective hypnotic apathy and credulity in an audience that was rapidly losing, for a time, its power of independent thought.

Mr. Stead's Explanation

Mr. Stead rose at once and explained what had occurred at his house, and said that "he knew the speaker and his wife, and that, *quite unknown to themselves*, they really were most remarkable mediums. No notice need therefore be taken of the man's words. Not only so, but he had only that day received an important communication from Mr. F. W. H. Myers (who has 'passed over') to the effect that he was watching this particular séance with the deepest interest, and that it would prove very remarkable." Moreover, Mr. Stead pointed out the unprecedented precautions against all fraud; so we might know that all that we saw would be genuine. I was stunned, and looked at all the undisturbed faces with amazement, until I recalled Dr. Bramwell's demonstration, and then I began to understand why NO ONE spoke or moved, or even smiled.

We Enter the Cabinet

Still the "spirits" were obdurate, and the man complained there was not sufficient magnetism in the room. So it was suggested that while we were waiting for the "power" we should enter the cabinet in couples, holding each other's hands, to see there was no fraud (!) and that the medium alone was there—who, of course, had heard all that transpired. It was obvious to me that such a move gave any confederate in the audience the needed opportunity to introduce anything wished for into the "cabinet." However, we went, two by two, with great solemnity and returned to our seats, assuring Mr. Stead we had seen nothing inside but the woman. When it was my turn to go in, I said to her "Do your best"; and in a strong accent, similar to her husband's, she replied, "Oh, that's all right. I'll give you a good show."

The Materialisation

We then sung another hymn or jubilee song, while the gas was lowered still further; and then——in the gloom, on the floor just where the curtains met, I saw what looked like a pool of quicksilver. This slowly climbed up as the curtains parted, until at last I realised that what I saw was a silvery foot and leg (evidently luminous paint). There was no mist or indistinctness; all had a hard, sharp outline, though dimly seen. Slowly the curtains kept on dividing, and a female form gradually emerged, clad in a thin gauze wrap; and eventually the curtains dropped behind her, and the supposed materialised spirit stood within six feet of me, a gleaming, shining white figure.

The silence was intense; even the "jubilee song" had died down in the solemn hush, and then the voice of Mr. Stead was heard explaining, in low, quiet tones, that he recognised the figure as that of a dear deceased relative—I think it was his aunt—and explained the wonders of materialisation we were privileged to witness. "There was the figure," he said, pointing to the apparition, "and all the time the medium was sitting on her kitchen chair in the 'cabinet.'"

The Second Sensation

But the "Society Entertainer" would not stand this, and then occurred the *second* great sensation of the afternoon. "No, I AIN'T," said the figure in a loud voice with a strong American accent, "I'M HERE."

It was awful, and I mus tsay I now awaited a tremendous explosion of wrath. But by this time the power of "collective hypnotism," aided perhaps by the old maxim "*populus vult decipi*," maintained an absolute silence in the room, and the figure slowly withdrew, no doubt recognised by other skilled observers as one of *their* relatives. Three times did the figure appear, and gradually disappear. All appeared profoundly interested. Mr. Stead, who seemed to know the procedure beforehand, and yet who, I am persuaded, acted in perfect (hypnotised) good faith throughout, then announced that any who wished might now go up to the curtains and peep through them.

A Piteous Sight

So at last, after two hours, our hands were loosed, and one and another went and peered in, and believed that they saw the luminous presentment of some loved one who had "passed over." It was piteous. I sat still and, after half an hour, the curtains were suddenly burst open, and out rushed (in her blouse, skirt, stockings, and shoes again) the medium in an apparent trance. I caught her and said "Bravo!" "I did it all right, didn't I?" said she.

Of course, on the principle of better late than never, I expected some leading man in the room now to say something to the point. But no! They broke up amicably, and the fragments of conversation I heard pointed to the belief they had had a very remarkable and interesting spiritist séance.* I wrote to Mr. Stead, saying the method employed by the performers was perfectly obvious; that when the "cabinet" was visited a small roll of

---

* Here, and in Mr. Stead's action, is shown the remarkable fact that after the hypnotic effect has gone the delusion still persists in good faith, being established in the brain as a demonstrated truth.

gauze and some luminous paint could be readily introduced, and that it ought to be exposed. To my surprise, Mr. Stead was furious, and asked how I dared suspect any of *his* audience, that if any one brought apparatus *it must have been myself*(!)

Approval of F. W. H. Myers

"None, however," he said, "had been brought; and he had already had a communication from (the much harassed) Mr. F. W. H. Myers to congratulate him on the successful séance," which he (Mr. Stead) declared was the most wonderful materialisation ever seen in London (this was probably true), etc., and he also said he had many letters of congratulation from the audience. This finally demonstrated the amazing truth that Mr. Stead and distinguished scientists in my presence had deliberately preferred to accept the evidence of their own hypnotised senses than to believe the testimony of the performers themselves. I doubt that it is possible to give stronger evidence of "collective hypnotism." Comment is needless; but the sadness, to me, of seeing a company of distinguished savants deceived by such puerile methods was naturally much mitigated by being able to attribute their attitude to "collective hypnotism."

Six Drunken Mediums

I am told, however, by a well-known "Christian" occultist, Mr. Robert King, that materialisation of "spirits" does take place; and that in this country there are at least six mediums who can effect it, but that one and all are drunkards and will resort to trickery if they possibly can, as being so much easier and more certain, which one can well imagine. Of course, this may or may not be true; but, in view of my experience, it is obvious that the greatest care is needed to exclude delusions. It is only, perhaps, fair to add that Sir O. Lodge did not agree with Mr. Stead in the genuineness of the phenomena; and Mr. Stead had to call in the testimony "from the other side" of the hard-worked Mr. F. W. H. Myers in his support. Mr. Myers said he had read a report of the meeting in the *Daily Chronicle*; whether this is a compliment to the journal or the reverse, we must leave the editor to decide.

I have never heard any one doubt it was the best materialising séance seen in London, and yet soon after the husband and wife were showing similar phenomena to any one at 2s. 6d. a head!

More Wonderful Still

But after all, I sometimes wonder whether even the amazing instance I have given illustrates the power of collective hypnotism so powerfully as an event well known to us all, and yet never scientifically accounted for. I allude to the supposed presence of thousands of Russian soldiers all over England at the close of 1914.

Here we get, not an "hysterical" crowd massed together for some common object, holding hands and singing hymns in the dark, and ready to believe almost anything, but men of the highest standing and utmost probity, accustomed to weigh their words, women of the highest honor isolated in country houses, or citizens keeping solitary watches

as special constables all over England and Scotland—
in short, a whole nation, not of imaginative Celts,
but of cold-blooded, slow-minded Anglo-Saxons, all
involved in one common gigantic delusion, which
was believed by them so implicity that to doubt
their word was to court their severe displeasure and
to write oneself a fool.

It was not that they all saw or heard the same
thing; they did not.

The Same Lie

But they one and all believed the same lie!
Not that any authority ever told this lie; but it
sprang up practically almost of itself in a night, and
in twenty-four hours seemed common property,
all over England, with a few doubters at a heavy
discount.

Grave parsons had heard crowds, with their
bearded heads out of the carriage windows, talking
and shouting Russian as they slowly passed some
wayside station. My brother-in-law, as a special
constable in Middlesex, told me he had special
warning to guard two bridges as the Russian Army
trains were to pass that night. Another cousin in
Somerset watched a long train full of Russians
slowly pass under the road bridge below his house.
An interesting letter from Aberdeen told me of four
long trains full of Russians which had been despatched
south that night, holding up the ordinary traffic.
These had come from Archangel!

Another helped to give refreshments to the
Russians at a wayside station, and another saw
thousands off at the docks. I might go on for

pages, but I doubt not that each of my readers can give just as good instances of this gigantic national hypnosis as I can.

Sanity no Protection

No falsehood seemed too great to believe, and no person too truthful to tell it. No amount of sanity seemed a sufficient protection against the over-whelming delusion. Surely anything in "collective hypnotism" at séances or elsewhere is easily possible after this.

The belief moreover was not vague, it was circumstantial; it gave dates and places, the smallest and most accurate details, and even sketches of what never occurred, and was never heard nor seen —only believed in. The hallucination was universal!

Consider the circumstances. Our forces were retreating; the dreaded Huns were at our throats. The fall of Paris was but a matter of a very short time, the Government already having left it. England had strained every nerve to place adequate forces in the field; but all were too few, all was insufficient, there was no help.

When, suddenly, there was light in the darkness! "The Russians were coming!" "But how?" for European travel was impossible. "Direct from Archangel" came the reassuring answer, and England drew one long breath of relief. "Yes, they were coming! In thousands, in tens of thousands, in hundreds of thousands!"

Seeing the Invisible

And so all the sober-minded men and women went forth to welcome them, and hear and see them; and they did all three.

They stood on the bridges and cheered the Russians that weren't there. They saw in thousands men that did not exist, and heard Russian tongues everywhere, which were nowhere. And yet to doubt their word, to tell the smallest vestige of the truth, was to be a traitor of the deepest dye, unworthy of the society of honest Englishmen.

"Thank God, they could believe their own eyes and ears," and they did; and they now know with what result.

From this it would appear that a hallucination may persist for days (or years?), and small details (when under a false belief) may be seen and recorded by men of the highest standing, that absolutely were never seen and never existed. In short, the "Russian legend" is the most complete proof of the possible unreality of all phenomena accounted real in Spiritism. The rejoinder, of course, is that nothing can then be proved as true or real. The reply can only be, "You must judge each individual case on its own merits. Consider the Russians; apply the conditions; and in examining the supposed phenomena bear these in mind, and apply such tests, as your ingenuity suggests, that will exclude every form of hallucination by 'collective hypnotism' or otherwise."

Another Instance

When you have done all this you will agree with me that the terrible strides of modern science have, indeed, made it very hard for modern Spiritism to establish their "facts."

To produce them, after all, is now only half the battle. It must not be imagined that the "Russian legend" is the only instance of "collective hypnotism." On the contrary, they occur all over the country, quite commonly. On May 26th, 1907, over one hundred people in France, men and women, declared on oath that they had seen large oval hailstones, each bearing the image of the Virgin.

Of course, the most puzzling cases to reason in the long list of Spiritist phenomena are the floating of D. D. Home in and out of a window, eighty-five feet above the ground, in Buckingham Gate; and the long series of appearances of "Katie King" in Sir Wm. Crookes' rooms—a supposed materialised spirit.*

Hypnosis Does Not Account for All

Sir Wm. Barrett ("On the Threshold of the Unseen," p. 37) says that "when fraud does not explain the phenomena, and when the observers are such as Sir Wm. Crookes, Professor de Morgan and others, the witnesses thought they saw what they described owing to some hallucination of the senses, such as occurs in "incipient hypnosis" (if for "incipient" Sir Wm. Barrett had written "col-

* Much doubt, however, is thrown on "Katie King" by the fact that the medium Florence Cook has been convicted of fraudulent materialization. See p. 193.

lective," he would have represented my theory), "but," he continues, "*I found the facts completely shattered my theory.*

"In many cases all preconceived theories of fraud, and illusions, and mal-observation must be abandoned,"

Well! Be it so. Still, "collective hypnotism" accounts for much. I have never thought it accounted for all. I have always held that when science and scepticism have done their best to destroy the credibility of the facts (not the theories) of Spiritism, there remains an indestructible residuum which is the work (so far as we at present know) of non-human agencies; and which, personally, I believe to be spirits of another world, but certainly not disembodied spirits of the dead.

CHAPTER X

DANGERS OF SPIRITISM

Peril not Exaggerated

I HAVE already throughout this book at times spoken of the dangers attaching to modern Spiritism; and some may think that enough has already been said upon the subject.

Lately, moreover, there has been a determined effort on the part of Spiritists to pour ridicule on such warnings, and the new leaders are very forward in declaring these perils are grossly exaggerated, and that people need not be alarmed; the good far outweighing the evil, and so on.

Older and more experienced members of the cult do not write like this. On the contrary, I have been astonished at the candour and earnestness with which these men of high integrity write about the great dangers that beset the very study they are advocating. Professor Flournoy says that his opposition to Spiritism is due "to its harmful effects—moral, mental, and physical."

To me, alas, the subject has become a very painful one, since it has touched my own friends.

Personal Experience

It is when one sees one of the finest cavalry officers in the British Army, one of one's own circle, a clever and brave man, driven out of his senses by it that one begins to understand what "playing with fire" means. For, with every desire to speak with truth and moderation, I consider that any dabbling with Spiritism, even in the most innocent beginnings, means nothing less than this.

It would be criminal for me, then, with such beliefs and such experiences, to omit this chapter; and I do not for one moment think Spiritists of real experience will blame me for recording my evidence of the dangers of this occult study.

These dangers may broadly be considered under the two heads of causes and classes. In medicine, in the study of disease, we have always what we call the predisposing cause, that which indirectly produces it; and the exciting cause, to which the disease is directly due.

Predisposing Cause

What I would call the predisposing cause of danger in Spiritism is the same as it is in disease, the personality and history of the sufferer.

The special evil in Spiritism is that it is just those unstable natures which are most attracted by its tenets and practices, which are those to whom it is the greatest danger. All are not equally exposed to risk. Which are those natures who are? Chiefly highly strung, imaginative and credulous people, men and women, of a more or less weak, nervous temperament. The majority at séances are, as a rule, individuals of this class.

It must be remembered that when we speak of millions of Spiritists we include all the "camp-followers" of the army; we include thousands who have no real interest in the subject, and never go further than table-turning. And though sporadic cases suffer, even amongst these, they are not the class who encounter the real dangers; for I have already pointed out, in table-turning and such elementary practices, that the danger is not in the practice itself, but in what it leads to.

The Acute Reader

Those who get absorbed in Spiritism are just those unstable natures which are prone to disaster. It is these that feel most strongly the almost irresistible attraction of Spiritism. Seeing, as I do continually, this especial class, I am quite sure that no patient of mine ought to ever dabble in this pursuit. And yet some do, and I greatly fear for them, and do my best to help them. I hope they will read this book.

"Now," says the acute reader, "the man has unmasked himself! Here is no fair judgment of Spiritism. Under an appearance of presenting both sides of a subject, a violent opponent of the cult writes this book, with its distorted contents. No doubt, what the doctor here says is true enough in itself. It *is* these very nervous and unbalanced people who do the noble cause of Spiritism so much harm. But certainly he is not the man to write about it"; and so on.

One can understand the diatribe; but the book, after all, must be judged on its merits, and not by the profession of its writer. At first sight one would hardly have thought a well-known writer of fiction could become the best exponent of Spiritism—but such a verdict would be most unfair.*

Fifty Years of Study

I have ever, as my friends know, been an earnest student of psychological problems, and for nearly fifty years of those specially associated with Spiritism, my interest being first awakened by the case recorded on p. 44, which I met in my Guernsey college days.

Moreover, it is quite clear that my present chapter is endorsed, at any rate in its purpose, by the most experienced Spiritists, so that it may be said, indirectly, to promote the true interests of Spiritism.

The principal objections I have to this modern cult have yet to be urged, and will be found set forth in Chapter XII. These have, however, no connection at all with my profession, directly or indirectly, but are on different grounds altogether, as the reader will see.

A Fair Presentation

Such objections would be only weakened by any untrue picture of that which I condemn. I have therefore endeavoured, by special research, to present the subject from the point of view of Spiritists themselves, rather than from my own; and for this reason I think I have been rather more than fair in presenting my facts.

No doubt, if this book had been written with any

* After all, the subject is not wholly uncongenial to the creator of Sherlock Holmes, for it certainly is full of both mystery and fiction.

literary skill, this "*apologia*" would have its rightful place in the preface; but that must pass; and perhaps, after all, being where it is, it may better clear the air for our present subject. This chapter is no pronouncement whatever, good or bad, on the cult of Spiritism, which is veritably fast becoming a new religion, and will, I feel sure, soon be proclaimed as such by others besides Conan Doyle; but solely a warning of the real dangers, physical, mental and moral (rather than spiritual), which beset its votaries. This last class of danger I leave at present, as it will be fully considered in Chapter XII.

No Tampering

"There are," says Professor Flournoy, "principles and powers, which we, in our ignorance, toy with; without knowing the frightful consequences which may result from tampering with the unseen world."*

It is, I think, obvious that those whose heredity or temperament indicates any tendency to nervous instability should keep absolutely clear from any such "tampering."

But besides the "predisposing cause" of temperament, there are at least two exciting or direct causes of any subsequent trouble, which may be pointed out.

No one can blame Spiritism for the "temperament" of its students, but all its best friends will join me in my warnings.

Exciting Cause

One exciting cause is common to all students, and that is, that Spiritism itself, in its very nature, con-

* "Spiritism and Psychology," p. 9.

tinually occupies our minds with much that is not only mystic, but positively unwholesome; and in doing so, it calls forth and uses many of the latent powers of humanity, as "telepathy," telekinesis(?), clairvoyance and clairaudience, hypnotic conditions, and the prominent action of the unconscious mind.

Now most of these, and possibly other latent powers, are possessed in varying degree by large numbers who are unconscious of them; and as their development and their continued use and cultivation is *at present* more or less of a danger, the risk is very widely spread.

Latent Powers

It seems to me possible, and, from my experience, very probable that we possess certain latent senses or powers far transcending in force those that we at present use, and which are dimly seen in uncertain ways by some on rare occasions. Spiritism is the special cult which vigorously stimulates the use of these very powers. But this, without doubt, often proves very unsafe. I believe that at present these powers should be allowed to lie dormant, and should not be called into active or constant use. "We are not what we shall be," and "we know not what we shall be," but there can be no doubt that a time will come when every power we possess will be fully developed and used.

There are at present very few who have developed these powers to any great extent who have not suffered more or less from doing so. This is true of nearly every medium* over the whole world, each

* Curiously enough, earnest students constantly end in becoming "mediums" themselves.

one of whom cultivates, and many of whom live by, the exercise of these rare powers. The tendency in such is ever downwards. The body physically seems, sooner or later, unable to bear the strain; the mind, in like manner, seems to lose its fibre, its will power, its concentration; the moral character markedly deteriorates; drunkenness and other vices prevail; and the whole condition becomes more or less deplorable.

Disastrous Results

Such disastrous results do not follow the use of any of our normal powers. I think, then, that I am fully justified in believing, on evidence that cannot be denied, that we are not intended at present to develop or actively use these wounderful powers, while at the same time we cannot but believe there will be hereafter conditions in which they will prove of the greatest service, very possibly in that "other world" Spiritists seem so anxious to discover.

My testimony regarding the moral, mental, and physical deterioration produced is entirely derived from Spiritists.

The other exciting cause is only experienced by the few who penetrate deeply into the secrets of the "séance." Perhaps I can best point it out in other words than my own.

I have already quoted Professor Flournoy, who clearly indicates their dangers.

They come, as he plainly shows, from the other world, and I shall proceed to show, more in detail, what these special dangers are.

This, indeed, brings me to the second part of my

subject—the classes of dangers to which we are exposed in Spiritism.

Seven in Number

These are seven in number:—

1. The moral and religious dangers.
2. The dangers to reason.
3. The dangers of "possession."
4. The loss of will power.
5. The dangers associated with necromancy.
6. The physical dangers.
7. The dangers of imposition.

1. Respecting moral and religious dangers, I shall consider the former here only; the latter will not be touched on now, being best left to the twelfth chapter.

A. P. Sinnett's experience of the records of life after death are very terrible and lowering to the moral sense. They are mostly so grossly sensual and obscene that he cannot possibly put his experiences into words, as he plainly states. This is by no means an isolated experience.*

Instances of Danger

Mrs. Forbes, a secretary of the S.P.R., lost her son, and, overwhelmed with grief, sought to get a communication with him. She soon spoke to what she thought was her son daily; and then suddenly, one night, had a most dreadful experience with a "man," or some powerful spirit who had forced himself (from the other world) into her presence,

* The horrible and obscene revelations of "juju" in East Africa point to a similar state of things in the devil worship there. It's rather too much to have this imported into England!

through the medium of automatic writing. For a very similar case see Mr. E. F. Benson's recent remarkable book, "Across the Stream." It is, of course, fiction, but is a most truthfully drawn picture of the real thing I am alluding to.

Dr. Thornton's daughter, using the planchette, got responses from a spirit which had not given its name. She said, "If you can't write your name, make a cross." Then the planchette seemed seized with a fury, and swept away from the hands upon it.* Miss Thornton put it back, and she again said "Make a cross." It wrote on the paper, in letters six inches long, "No, No, No!" "Make a cross or go," she replied. Then it wrote "Curse you," and left.

I fear this savours of the melodramatic; but I cannot help it, as I believe the story to be authentic, and there really seems a good deal of "melodrama" in Spiritism!

Will any say that such beings are not a very real danger both to faith and morals?

Immorality

A steady teacher in a board school, thirty-six years of age, a single man, of temperate habits in all things, began to dabble in spirit-writing, and soon was answered by a most unclean spirit writing the most obscene words and suggesting the most wicked thoughts and drawing awful pictures. It gradually destroyed his character, and he entered on a dissolute life, spending his time and money in orgies of debauchery.

---

* We have also accounts from Sir Wm. Crookes and others of the apparent "possession" of inanimate objects.

Some years ago Dr. Egbert Muller left Spiritism and became a Roman Catholic. His conviction (1900) of the character of Spiritism, after many years of experience and investigation, is that it is a bold scheme for the destruction of Christianity. Dr. B. F. Hatch, with but little inquiry, came across seventy immoral mediums. I have already shown that all materialising mediums a few years ago were reputed drunkards and liars.* The dangers to reason are perhaps even greater than to morals.

Many Lunatics

2. Dr. Forbes Winslow (not the author) is responsible for the statement that 10,000 were then (1877) in asylums, victims to Spiritism. Such a statement is extremely difficult to verify; but, at any rate, it represents the opinion of an expert alienist.

Of course, neuropathic patients, as I have shown, yield most readily to artificial somnambulism or the medium trance, and hence are most easily drawn into Spiritist practices, and it is these whose "reason" is most readily endangered.

We find, indeed, in those whose reason is most seriously injured for life there is generally (not always) some hereditary history of an adverse nature. A leading Spiritist, C. Flammarion, says: "It is prudent not to give oneself exclusively to occult subjects, for one might soon lose the independence of mind necessary to form an impartial judgment."

It is most unfortunate that Spiritism should

* It might be pointed out here that it is acknowledged by experts that the moral standard of the unconscious mind (always active in séances) is much lower than that of the conscious.

attract the unstable in this way, to whom it does so much harm.

Danger to Sensitives

A member of the S.P.R., writing on "The Dangers of Spiritism," says that "undeniable sensitives (with psychic and mediumistic gifts), apart from money, are endangered not only in séances, but in private investigations." It must not, however, be supposed, on the other hand, that a well-balanced mind makes Spiritism safe; for it does not.

A lady living in Devonshire conducted, from the age of sixteen, all sorts of Spiritist phenomena, which nearly cost her her reason, and left her a hopeless cataleptic. A very clever Spiritist leader died in an asylum in Paris the other day. He was well known to me. Innumerable other cases could be given; and a friend, whose brother was one of the best known Spiritists in America, told me that his brother did not know of a single case where the study had been pursued without distinct deterioration of the mental, moral, or spiritual faculties ensuing. Continued "possession" by an evil spirit nearly always ends in chronic mental disease. The results of automatic writing are perhaps the more dangerous to reason, physical phenomena being comparatively harmless.

The continued use of supposed necromancy is very easy, and very common; but it is constantly followed by painful and dangerous results to the reason.

I have already alluded to a most painful case of a cavalry officer that fell a victim to the Bureau of

Julia, established by Mr. Stead, and which, I fear, is by no means a solitary example.

He went there in all innocence, in great grief, having recently lost his mother, and soon got into (supposed) touch with her; and then the interviews became more and more frequent, but with most disastrous results. One day, on the parade ground, he gave a series of ridiculous orders, and he was brought home a lunatic. He tried to kill his aged father that night, obsessed by the vision of his mother; and it was my melancholy duty to take him, the next day, to a suitable retreat, a total loss to the Army of one of their bravest and most efficient officers.

With regard to the dangers of "possession," I have already given some remarkable instances of this condition, so that what I refer to is well understood: for I believe that now, in this twentieth century, there are cases in our asylums as clearly those of "possession" by unclean spirits as ever there were on the shores of the Sea of Galilee in our Saviour's time.

The Rev. Cyril E. Hudson, in the *Nineteenth Century* for May, 1919, says: "Spiritists know that if you rend the thin veil which separates this world from the next, you can have no guarantee whatever as to the character of the personalities which will avail themselves of the rent. You are running an awful risk."

"It is simply puerile," says another, "to refuse to face the possibility that evil spirits may rush to the threshold when the door is opened."

A writer in the *Occult Review* says: "Spiritists

are well aware of the awful peril of 'obsession' by evil spirits. Man has some very dangerous and powerful enemies behind the veil."

3. A boy of twenty-five, dabbling in Spiritism, narrowly escaped "possession," being saved by a wise friend, a member of the S.P.R. (which must never be confounded with Spiritism, as it holds no dogmas, advances no opinions, and teaches no creed), though there was a fearful struggle before it could be accomplished. "A hundred hands seemed to be battering at the walls, ceiling, and all the furniture, while the boy and his friend sat paralysed with fear in the bedroom, the servants having all gone, terrified with fear, to bed." "What ten minutes was in that bedroom," the friend says, "cannot be imagined! It seemed as though the very rabble of the unseen world had been let loose, in order to exhibit to us the power of its malice, and of its (fortunately) impotent rage!"

As a rule, in "possession," the awful truth is that it is the spirit that is the seeker after the man, and not the man after the spirit. Only in rare cases, when the spirit comes in some lovely and bewitching form, is the latter the case. On some occasions the entry into the personality is effected quite suddenly and insidiously.*

4. The next danger, "loss of will power," is undoubtedly a contributory cause to "possession." Sir William Barrett well says with regard to this: "Spiritism is dangerous in proportion as it leads us

---

* A comparison between this awful hunt for the soul and the "Hound of Heaven" affords a wonderful glimpse of the forces of evil and good striving for the soul of man.

to surrender our reason or our will to the dictates of an invisible and often lying being."

Dr. Marcel Viollet describes how this occurs: "In a séance no one knows if anything will happen, and all are reduced to a condition of nerve tension before anything occurs.

"Eyes and ears are strained to know what is going to happen at the little table where the medium sits"; and it is when in this condition, and when the little table begins to speak, that the weakened will is so often subservient to the spirit.

In the Agapemone, an immoral religious body in the south of England (to turn for one moment from Spiritism), the head was Mr. H. J. Prince, who was a man of prayer and self-denial, with a perfectly upright private life. His fall was undoubtedly due to the absolute yielding of his will to supposed spirit guidance, putting on one side the plain teaching of the Bible and the voice of common sense. "He no longer needed these helps," in his own judgment, "on account of his full surrender to what he thought was the Spirit of God." Alas! it was something far different, and soon led him into the most debased life and practices.* When once the mind and will are voluntarily surrendered (the citadel is impregnable until we yield up its custody), neither shrewdness nor faith will save us from the dangers of seducing spirits. The surrender of free-will in Spiritism is most dangerous, and also most common.

Raupert, in "Modern Spiritism," says (p. 72): "Much passivity indeed would seem to be the key-

---

* This notorious scandal was known everywhere—but not its cause.

note of all spiritual experience, and the end by which the spirit world most efficiently carries on its operations on the psychic plane."

The danger of automatic writing is very great, inasmuch as it necessarily involves the absolute yielding of one's hand to an unknown power and being; and it is thus that this is, perhaps, the most frequent beginning of "possession." As Sir Wm. Barrett remarks, "In Spiritism we lose our individuality."

Dr. H. Maudsley says: "It is impossible to escape the penalty of weakening the will"; and, since complete passivity is an essential in all Spiritist séances, it is easily seen how readily will-power becomes lessened and eventually lost. Sir Oliver Lodge very gravely says: "Self-control is more important than any other form of control, and whoever possesses the power of receiving communications in any form should see to it that he remains master of the situation. To give up your own judgment and depend solely on adventitious aid is a grave blunder, and may in the long run have disastrous consequences. Moderation and common sense are required in those who try to utilise powers which neither they nor any fully understand, and a dominating occupation in mundane affairs is a wholesome safeguard."

Once one begins to practise Spiritism one cannot say where one may end, and herein lies its greatest peril; its very mystery and interest insensibly draw its votaries on. It seems to exercise an extraordinary fascination, which seems to demand the very full self-surrender against which we are so often warned.

For our comfort let us remember that there can be, as I have said, no invasion of our human personality without our own consent.

Only in great moderation, and in retaining full self-control of ourselves, is any measure of safety to be found.

5. What I feel, having written thus far, is that no arguments are needed to justify to the full the very severe way in which Divine wisdom has forbidden all such intercourse with the unseen world as is deliberatedly courted in Spiritism. I only touch on this point here, as it is my subject later on.

It seems strange that the same voice of Spiritism should, with one breath, candidly acknowledge the great dangers surrounding the practice of necromancy and, with the next, scoff at the solemn warnings of Scripture against them. "Not for nothing," says C. E. Hudson, in the *Nineteenth Century*, "has the Church throughout her history discouraged the practice of necromancy, the morbid concern with the dead which must inevitably interfere, and does in fact interfere, with the proper discharge of our duties in that plane of existence in which God has placed us."

The special evils of necromancy are pointed out in the *Times* of July 9th, 1908. It says: "After every effort (to the contrary) theory came round to the ancient explanation that the baffling personality is a spirit, some sort of dæmon. When we die are we then to join the wordy rabble, whose jargon does not seem as a rule like revelations of the secrets of the prison-house, but rather more like gibberings from a lunatic asylum, peopled by inmates of vulgar behaviour, and of the lowest morals; creatures that lie and cheat, give false names and unverifiable addresses?" and, I may add, make the most nauseous and vilest puns. Some of these, I regret to say, greatly disfigure Sir Oliver Lodge's book "Raymond."

The *British Quarterly Review* says: "To hearken to the voice of the dead is either a delusion or a reality. If it be the former, no delusion can be more mischievous, more degrading, more revolting. If it be the latter, no pursuit can be more dangerous."

And so we are left on the horns of this uncomfortable dilemma!

We recall Tennyson's lines in "In Memoriam":—

"How pure of heart, and sound of head,
    With what divine affections bold,
    Should be the man whose thoughts would hold
    An hour's communion with the dead."

6. Turning now to the sixth class of danger, "the physical," we find it is one that is least understood. My attention was first called to it some years ago, when staying with a lady who was fond of Spiritism.

She complained to me very much of the extreme exhaustion she felt after attending séances, and wondered whether it was due to parting with some portion of her flesh. as well as her vitality, in the process of materializing spirits (to say nothing of the clothing which, we are assured, is derived in fragments from the audience).

Since then I have known more of the extreme physical exhaustion of mediums, and the great physical self-sacrifice with which they pursue their doubtful and dangerous profession. Sometimes, indeed, we have evidence that this amounts to real physical danger to life.

Professor Hudson (of America) states that the exercise of Spiritism "produces physical deterioration which keeps pace with mental decline; and which, no doubt, loosens all principles of morality and truth." Mediums are peculiarly exposed to these dangers, and yet Sir A. Conan Doyle writes, in "The New Revelation": "Nearly every woman is an undeveloped medium. Let her try her own powers of automatic writing." Sir A. Conan Doyle has already rightly been taken to task as a doctor for giving such dangerous and unprofessional advice.

7. This last of the evil effects of Spiritism is the result of being continually in the atmosphere of fraud and folly. At first, doubtless, one is healthily disgusted and revolts against it. By degrees, however, this feeling wears away (I think the subtle process can be discerned in "Raymond"), and the mind, first of all, gets accustomed to the lowering atmosphere, and eventually tries to justify it as a necessary accompaniment of the marvellous revelations. The whole ends in unmistakably degrading the character of a large majority of those who have given themselves up to the practice of Spiritism. Swedenborg, in his "Spiritist Diary" (sec. 1622), says: "Let them who speak with spirits beware lest they be deceived when they say that they are those whom they know, or pretend to be."

Sir A. Conan Doyle goes so far as to own that "There are, I think, deliberate frauds, either from this side or the other" (or from both).

For a most interesting *exposé* of frauds of inconceivable skill by which sealed letters are opened and read, pendulums locked in glass cases moved at will, rappings produced anywhere, writing on closed and locked and untouched slates, flowers and toys materialised and scattered everywhere, the materialisation of the dead, the production of lights, of music, and of voices, let me strongly recommend "Behind the Scenes with the Medium" (330 pages), by David P. Abbott (Kegan Paul & Co., Ltd.), as a book from which the reader will rise a sadder, a disillusioned, and a wiser man.

Dr. Funk, a well-known figure in New York, and a foremost man in all psychological problems, and in Spiritism, says: "People are being fooled by thousands by the shallowest tricks at Spiritist séances."

Mediums, indeed, are mostly consciously fraudulent; a reliable one is an untold and very rare treasure to the investigator.

As I have shown, this is not so much because they love fraud, as because the power they possess is so capricious, and so often fails them at the critical moment, that they have no alternative but to resort to fraud to produce the phenomena for which the audience have paid and are impatiently waiting.

Eusapia Palladino, who is, I belive, a chief source of the belief in Spiritism of Sir Oliver Lodge, Myers, Professors Schiaparelli and Lombroso, is known, as already stated, frequently to have practised fraud of a glaring kind. Miss Florence Cook, the medium who produced Katie King for Sir William Crookes, was convicted of fraud in producing a lady of Queen

Anne's Court, and also when her materialised
"Mary" was seized and exposed.

I have now gone briefly through seven varieties of
dangers that are constantly found in Spiritism, of
which such fraud is one. All of these dangers are
more familiar to Spiritists and students of the subject
than they are to most of my readers.

Mrs. Sidgwick, for example, says: "I am afraid
'Raymond' is likely to lead many of such ignorant
people, who had much better not do so, to go to
professional mediums, and is likely to increase a very
undesirable trade."

I will conclude this rather depressing, but most
necessary, chapter with a few general remarks on my
subject.

Mr. E. Maitland was convinced at a Spiritist
séance that he was a reincarnation of St. John;
while one communication he received was from the
angel Gabriel. (Curious to say, my reader's surmise
is wrong, he was *not* mad.) Mr. J. Arthur Hill,
a well-known writer on Spiritism, remarks: "This
kind of thing is dangerous. Avoid automatic
writing unless you are prepared to treat everything
with a critical sceptical scrutiny.

"There does seem something very diabolic in the
heartless deception which they (the mediums) so
often perpetuate. I do not take the communications
seriously as regards their face value; but there is
always an element of danger (present)."*

The celebrated medium, D. D. Home, felt the
spirits that controlled him were gaining entire
mastery of his whole being, and gave up Spiritism

* "Spiritism," J. Arthur Hill, pp. 91, 92.

entirely, and joined the Roman Catholic Church (representing to him the orthodox Christian faith). The spirit control ridiculed his escape, but promised to leave him alone for one year. When this time was expired, Home resumed his séances, and gave a celebrated one before Napoleon III.

In 1881 Canon Wilberforce examined into Spiritism, and believed it to be a revival of pagan mysteries and practices. This probably contains more than a little truth; and, if so, it is extremely interesting and instructive, showing continuity of thought somewhere, in spite of the entire want of human connection between a New England family in Massachusetts and Eastern magic. It suggests, indeed, that the revival of Spiritist practices may be due rather to a continuity of thought and purpose in the other world than in this.

The Rev. W. Stainton Moses, the most upright medium ever known, who held the almost unique position of never being convicted of any fraud, was terribly assailed by dæmons (?), and eventually gave up the Christian faith entirely.

A member of the S.P.R. wrote some eighteen years ago on Spiritism for two purposes. He believed in, and sought to establish, "First: The reality of the phenomena. Second: The great danger of the whole pursuit." Unbelievers in these two are almost exclusively those who have not investigated the subject.

F. W. H. Myers has also expressed very forcibly his knowledge of the great dangers which are inseparable from Spiritism.

I could continue *ad nauseam*. Perhaps I have

already done so, to many of my readers. My apology must be that I don't want to recur to this subject.

I wish to present a truthful picture of the dangers, which are not accidental and occasional occurrences due to ignorance in controlling the phenomena; but which, on the contrary, are an essential factor of them; so that the greater the advance in the study, and the greater the experience, the greater the danger of "possession."

I wish to show that the terrible warnings of Scripture against all forms of necromancy, against all attempts of communication with another world, so far from being, as is so generally believed, the foolish prejudice of the infancy and ignorance of humanity, to be now dismissed with contempt by the matured wisdom and great knowledge of our time, are, to our dismay, justified on every side by actual scientific experiment.

Most now confess the phenomena real; also the experiments to prove the existence of spirits in another world, as well as the existence of the "other world" itself. True, it was not apparently necessary for any of our race to have recourse to this evidence, as our proud boast for ages has been in a Book which foretold all this, that we declared we believed was inspired, and we circulated it to all our more benighted brothers in millions (see reports of the British and Foreign Bible Society), and this Book was, as I have said, full of "the other world" and contained much information concerning the spirits inhabiting it.

I fear one could not urge that the studies of

Spiritists have been conducted with the pious idea of corroborating its statements, for all studies in necromancy are expressly forbidden, with what is now seen by modern science to be Divine wisdom, on account of their real danger to humanity.

The study of Spiritism, generally speaking, is apparently discouraged by all scientists who have investigated its wonders, and on the very remarkable ground that these are true, but unsafe to penetrate. It is undoubtedly condemned in principle and practice by the Bible, the "corner-stone of England's greatness" (see "Life and Letters of Queen Victoria"). Its researches are proved unnecessary to all believing Christians, who already know (by faith) more than it can ever reveal.

With such a history it does not seem too much to hope that the sober human mind will recover itself from the weak curiosity that ever gave Spiritism countenance, and justify its having arrived at the twentieth century of the faith and teaching of our great Lord and Master, by renouncing once more the Devil and all his works, in whatever subtle and specious form they may appeal to us, either through our curiosity or through our affections.

CHAPTER XI

THE FAILURES OF SPIRITISM

A Few Words Only

A few, only a very few, words on the subject of this chapter are needed if we are to have a complete picture of Modern Spiritism. It might, indeed, be thought by some that all through we have incidentally come across so many failures, and such very doubtful successes, that further exposure is unnecessary.

It may be so; yet remembering how very difficult it is to deliver and undeceive the obsessed, I venture to "pile it on" a little more; with the suggestion that the reader who is already sufficiently convinced might skip this short chapter. All others should read it for their own good.

With regard to séances, few have any idea how generally they fail to prove anything. Eusapia Palladino, the unrivalled medium of Naples, had in a short time twenty-seven séances where nothing happened. And yet she never scrupled to descend to fraud whenever it was necessary and possible. That skilled and reliable medium, the Rev. W. Stainton Moses, says that in ninety-nine out of one hundred séances people do *not* get what they want or expect. In short, séances are most unsatisfactory.

It must be remembered that failure to produce phenomena is better than their fraudulent imitation.

Paralysed Séances

Suspicion or scepticism (if known) seem as a rule fatal to the production of phenomena. Sympathy, without the critical faculty, seems essential. All changes in the ordinary procedure of a séance seem to paralyse it—a change of tables, an interruption by a sceptic, etc. It may be noted, in contrast, that our Lord's miracles were performed on occasions when rampant unbelief was present (St. Luke viii. 53; St. John xii. 37).

Trickery is common. Eusapia was exposed in America for fraud, and also in Italy. (Excuse repetition.) Mrs. Butler, a medium supported by Sir A. Conan Doyle, was twice convicted of fortune-telling.

White Eagle, a supposed North American Indian spirit "control," always spoke, like several others, for some unknown reason, in the negro dialect; while the two Thomases, well-known mediums, were both proved frauds.

In one séance with a masked medium the apparent materialisation of a spirit appeared so absolutely genuine that it was not until Mr. Sebil (the medium) admitted that its production was purely mechanical and the "clairvoyance" accompanying it sheer trickery, that its fraud was apparent.

False Statements

False statements from supposed spirits (of the dead) are so common as to be hardly worth recording.

Sir Walter Scott told Dr. Hodgson that he had seen a planet further from the sun than Saturn, and said its name was Mercury! George Eliot said, "I don't know as there is enough light to communicate."*

Dr. Funk, the well-known New York psychologist, in 1878 sat with Mrs. M. Fox Kane, one of the two Fox sisters (see Chapter II.) who started Modern Spiritism in 1847 by cracking their knee and finger joints to produce "spirit" raps, etc.

The spirit controlling the medium (Mrs. Kane) said, "I am John Seitz. I died nine days ago at Springfield, Ohio."

Two days after this Dr. Funk had another sitting with the same medium. Again the spirit said: "I am John Seitz. I died eleven days ago at Springfield, Ohio." Dr. Funk wrote to his sister, who replied John Seitz was alive and well.

The Non-existent Doctor

Dr. Phinuit, the celebrated spirit control of Mrs. Piper, who stated he was formerly a French doctor in Marseilles, has been shown not to be what he professed. He said he was born at Marseilles in 1790, and died in Paris in 1860. Enquiries fail to give any trace of him. He had no knowledge of medicine, and only appeared to know a few French phrases!

A Madame Dupont, a very respectable lady, received, through a medium, a message from "Rudolph," whom she knew, stating he had died at eleven that evening, and giving long details of his last hours. Then she had constant séances, at

* Quoted from *British Weekly*.

each of which "Rudolph's" spirit spoke to her of its experiences. These continued until a letter came from him stating, incidentally, that he was in perfect health.

Lately, Mr. J. Arthur Hill received communications from Professor Wm. James, Professor Lombroso, of Italy, from W. T. Stead, and from King Edward VII., stating that in July Great Britain would sink beneath the sea!

A Cruel Case

Warnings of coming disaster were given at a Spiritist séance to a man and his wife. Believing these to be true, they sold up their home and left Mexico, because the spirit had said the district would be destroyed by an earthquake. When they arrived in New York, nearly destitute, they attended another séance, and there the spirit told them they had been properly fooled, which was done just to show them they were to have "no concern with material things!"

Spiritism is sometimes called a science; but it has failed to make its claim good to such a title.

Professor Richet points out that Spiritist experience is in direct conflict with scientific accuracy and experience.

Spiritism not a Science

Their experiments do not give scientific results; for the more accurately and rigorously they are conducted, the fewer and more uncertain are the phenomena produced.

Moreover, and this is fatal to scientific claims, under similar conditions, the results obtained are far from being identical.* Sir A. Conan Doyle, though generally very dogmatic and credulous, is at times a keen critic. Respecting the famous cross-correspondence analyzed by Hon. Gerald Balfour in the S.P.R. (Ear of Dionysius) where two spirits of Greek scholars, Professors Verrall and Butcher, are supposed to collaborate, he says: "The spirits have the use of a very good library, or else they have memories something like omniscience. No human memory could possibly carry all the exact quotations which occur in these communications."

Professor Hyslop noted that with Mrs. Piper, when facts were asked for to prove the identity of the supposed "spirit," there was always great difficulty and hesitation in replying, although the medium was voluble and fluent before. Mrs. Sidgwick, sitting with Mrs. Piper in 1899, got in touch with Moses, the great lawgiver, who prophesied (falsely) a great war in the near future, in which England and America would fight France and Russia, and Germany would take no part.

A Spiritist writer states: "The force that moves ponderous objects without contact, either emanates from the spirits of the dead or from the living." Here is an unscientific statement in accounting for the physical phenomena; for it is more likely that the force emanates from neither, but from spirits (not discarnate) in another world.

Fraud Everywhere

Mr. W. T. Stead said that in the whole of the United Kingdom there was only one person† who

*This is most important when we consider its scientific claims.
† This was probably erroneous.

could materialise spirits, and who was of undoubted integrity—a Mrs. Mellor; and yet she was afterwards detected in the grossest fraud in Sydney.

Mr. Bishop, the well-known thought-reader, could give the contents of sealed envelopes with perfect ease, and had read them hundreds of times; but when Mr. Labouchere put a bank-note for a large sum of money in an envelope and offered it to Mr. Bishop if he could read the number of it, he failed to do so in spite of the most determined attempts. Only by this means was it discovered that his supposed power was a fraud.

In Spiritism, however, no such exposures seem to be a bar to faith. Many of the best phenomena it has produced are from convicted impostors.

Contradictory Necromancy

Turning to attempts at necromancy, we find the same trickery and fraud prevailing. These "departed spirits," as we have already shown, teach different and conflicting faiths in different countries. In France re-incarnation is taught; in England it is denied. It is thus found that the disembodied spirits of Kardec in France, of Stainton Moses in England, of Swedenborg in Sweden, of Mrs. Piper in America, give absolutely contradictory messages. No doubt this is accounted for by the phenomena of the unconscious mind and telepathy, which, of course, negatives "spirits." Andrew Lang does not believe in Mrs. Piper's communications with the dead, and "considers that all coming from her is worthless."

The spirits that love to personate great men—
Carlyle and Cardinal Newman—know nothing about
the books these have written; you find a Shake-
speare who can't spell; and a Bacon with no ideas
of anything. You find a Cardinal Newman who
knows no Latin, a Julius Cæsar ignorant of geog-
raphy, and a George Eliot who has forgotten her
grammar. In 1898, in a test case, when the spirit
of the Rev. Stainton Moses was professing to speak
to Mrs. Piper, it failed completely to disclose the
three secret names Mr. Moses had given to Mr. Myers
before he died.

The Desire to Believe

The Times reports that "in the course of some
amusing 'confessions' Professor Jacks (President
of the S.P.R.) emphasized the powerful influence
of the 'desire to believe,' and its overpowering influence on the exercise of common reason. 'While,
at times, it actually seemed as if he were communi-
cating with departed spirits, at others this feeling
was rudely broken by triviality and foolishness.'
He discussed the analogy of spirit-seeking with
dreams, and said 'that if a person once committed
himself to the statement that he believed in spirits
he would fight to the last ditch until every vestige
of regard for facts would be thrown to the winds.'"
One instinctively feels the truth of this.

The discarnate spirits of Melanchthon and of the
Catholic wife of Luther are both voluble in modern
German, which they never knew.

On December 13th, 1914, Sir Oliver Lodge and
the S.P.R. opened a sealed envelope written by

F. W. H. Myers in 1907 as a test, and compared it with what the medium had said was in it, and there was no resemblance whatever.

Messages from Myths

"It is just as easy," says Thoman Jay Hudson, "to obtain a communication from a living person (supposed to be dead) as from one actually dead, and just as easy from an imaginary as from an actual person."

Mr. Hudson has had very affectionate messages of a most touching nature from an imaginary sister, and also from himself, he being supposed to be at the time his own brother (while he was believed to have died years before). All the time he never had a brother or a sister! We make no comments on these facts, so disastrous to Spiritism; but before reaching our chapter on the relations of Spiritism to Christianity, we may draw our own conclusion on its relation to truth. That of others is well expressed in Mr. Frank Podmore's (S.P.R.) book: "*No positive results have been obtained worthy of record.*" My own opinion is as follows.

It is more than doubtful whether, in spite of its useless marvels and sustained efforts for half a century, Spiritism has revealed *any truth whatever* concerning another world or has had *any actual communication* with any departed spirit. Some things, as yet unaccounted for, are not sufficiently established as facts to invalidate these statements.

CHAPTER XII

SPIRITISM AND CHRISTIANITY

"Beloved, believe not every spirit, but prove the spirits whether they are of God."—1 JOHN iv. 1.

"But the Spirit saith expressly, that in latter times some shall fall away from the faith, giving heed to seducing spirits and doctrines of demons."—1 TIMOTHY iv. 1.

"And I saw coming out of the mouth of the dragon, and out of the mouth of the beast, and out of the mouth of the false prophet, three unclean spirits, as it were frogs: for they are spirits of demons, working signs."—REVELATION xvi. 13, 14.

Nothing Proved

HITHERTO we have examined Spiritism on rational grounds, and have found it is exceedingly probable that so far nothing has really been discovered, and nothing proved of the unseen or unknown; and the craving of unbelievers in Christianity to know the secrets of the other world has not been satisfied.

Christians have no such cravings, and where faith is operative and the revelation of another world and of life after death is clear and definite, they do not feel inclined to spend hours in doubtful company, witnessing untold absurdities, and listening to incoherent, blasphemous, or most commonplace utterances, from a more or less entranced woman (too often, I regret to say, of somewhat doubtful reputation), respecting either the mighty dead, or some loved but absent one.

Communion with the Dead

Their real communion in spirit with such is far better enjoyed in their common nearness to their beloved Lord, whose presence they trust their dear ones are now enjoying; and in such communion it is best realized how thin is the veil between those who live in the Lord and those who die in the Lord.

As we shall see, Spiritism may have a certain value for unbelievers; but first of all we must understand what Modern Spiritism really is. So far we have only examined its phenomena, physical and psychical. It will now be our business to examine its dogmas and its doctrines, its position as a new religion, and its claims as a new faith, worthy to supersede Christianity, which, to many of our modern "deep thinkers," has become entirely impossible and completely out of touch with the spirit of the age (we confess this latter is both possible and probable).

Spiritism then, we are told, is "the new interpretation of the spirit world established by communication with the dead (necromancy); as shown by psychic and physical phenomena." (This last, we have shown, cannot possibly prove anything of the sort.)

Spiritists generally believe that there are no spirits in the other world but those of the departed; in other words, that they are all human.

Spiritism Anti-Christian

"Spiritism," wrote Stainton Moses, "is a revolution (not simply a reform) from the Christian idea;

which is drawing out a lingering life, choked by the incubus of sacerdotalism, and human theology."

Sir Arthur Conan Doyle, some fifty years later, says: "The physical basis of all psychic belief is that the soul is a complete duplicate of the body, resembling it in the smallest particular, although constructed in some far more tenuous material. In death there is a complete separation between the two bodies, and life is carried on entirely by the lighter of the two."

It is probably useless to urge that science has not admitted this contention, and that the whole statement is pure dogmatism.

"When St. Paul said, 'a spiritual body,' he meant a body which contained the spirit, and yet was distinct from the old material body. That is exactly what psychological science has now shown to be true." (Refer back to Chapters IV. and VI. to show how "Raymond" and others contradict all that Sir Conan Doyle here teaches.)

The Spiritist Dogma

The seven principles of the Spiritist dogma are said to be :—

1. The fear of God.
2. The brotherhood of man.
3. Continuous existence.
4. The communion of saints.
5. Present responsibility.
6. Compensation and retribution for good or ill.
7. A path of endless progress.

There are also seven spheres of probation (Theosophic). There is the rejection of good, which is the "one unpardonable sin" (!); and there is punishment for all sin. Spiritism thus becomes daily less and less of a scientific research, and more and more of a religion and a rival to Christianity.

It is found, practically, that a true Spiritist soon ceases to be, if indeed he ever was, in any ordinary sense of the word, a Christian.

Spiritists Non-Christians

Spiritism uncompromisingly rejects the leading doctrines of the Christian faith, including the "fall of man."

It is exultingly predicted that in ten years 50 per cent. of the civilised world will be Spiritist, a prospect which most will regard with very mixed feelings, and possibly some incredulity.

Spiritists exalt their lofty claims and aims, and declare that if the latter are really high and noble, they only attract high and noble spirits. It is somewhat remarkable, if there be any truth in this, that the reverse is what is generally observed. If one wants to see what is fraudulent, ignoble, and debased, it is, I fear, in a Spiritist séance that they may be most surely met with.

The Perispirit

Dr. Marcel Viollet, in 1910, says that "The Spiritist doctrine is that the soul in life is attached to the body by four or seven principles: one of which, called the 'perispirit' (astral body), clothes the soul after death. Later on the perispirit is re-incarnated (at any rate, in France) according to the Pythagorean theory. These souls (with their perispirits), good and bad, are all around us every-where." Such is the hypothesis of Spiritism. The astral body, more particularly, is said (with equal "truth") to be constructed of "bound" ether, which Fresnel and others have shown to be denser than "ordinary" ether (which is thousands of times denser than steel). Perhaps Sir Oliver Lodge may find time (if he has patience enough) to tell us if this be true. Sir Oliver observes that "there is after all, no great change in the next world, but all here appears less important. This," he says, "has been known over a century" (with regard to the latter half of the sentence he might have said "over nineteen").

A 50 per cent. Chance

W. T. Stead tells us that "Cecil Rhodes devoted much thought to the question whether or not there was a God" (such a question certainly requires a good deal of thought, even when of the capacity of a Cecil Rhodes), "and he came to the (somewhat lame) conclusion that there was a 50 per cent. chance that there was" (forgive the irreverence).

"Is there a similar chance," asks Stead, "that death does not end all." (More, I should say.)

"How then," he continues, "can we arrive at certainty." (We should suggest, by the same means that we are certain that Saturn has a ring, or Jupiter moons; that is, by faith in the evidence of others: in this case in the living God, who is more than a 50 per cent. chance to all reverent men.)

S.P.R. and Spiritism

There can be no doubt that with Spiritism must be closely associated (however little they like it) the S.P.R., whose annual volumes are now fully occupied in verifying (or otherwise) Spiritist phenomena. There can be no doubt that, though they do not blindly support it, or profess any opinions concerning it, they give a sort of semi-scientific "cachet" to its somewhat dubious proceedings that is still sorely needed. I am glad to be able to acknowledge here that on the ethical side, setting aside for the moment the immense harm it has done, Spiritism has done some good, but only to unbelievers.

It claims, indeed, that the "stupid materialism of yesterday has been exploded by the facts of Spiritism. The blind infidelity of the past has given place to a craving to get in touch with the realities of the unseen world." This witness is partly true; but, as I said, it is only "blind infidelity" that has been instructed; and not, I fear, in the "realities" of the unseen world," for these are, as I shall show, entirely unknown to Spiritism, but in the bare fact of its existence.

Holman Hunt and Ruskin

For instance, Holman Hunt said to Ruskin, "When last we met you declared you had given up all belief in immortality.

"I remember well," said Ruskin, "but what has mainly caused the change in my views is the unanswerable evidence of Spiritism. With this once proved I have no further interest in Spiritism."

The justification which Spiritism claims for its existence is the grossly exaggerated assertion that "a spirit world is everywhere denied." (This was never true, and since the decline of materialism, for the last fifty years, has become glaringly false.)

It is probable that, so far, Spiritism itself has been one of the factors in this decline of materialism (towards which, curiously enough, its (supposed) materialisations may have helped). One would imagine, however, to listen to its claims, that it was really responsible, as a sort of spiritual Columbus, for actually discovering a new world! There is not one word from these "discoverers" of apology to God or the Bible, for unbelief in their revelation of the very same truth, which, far from being brought to light by Spiritism, had been made known to all men since the present age began.

Survival after Death

The desire to verify survival after death is the inevitable outcome of loss of faith in revealed religion. To the humblest believer all the boasted discoveries of Spiritism which are true have ever been undoubted facts.

Professor Lombroso says he is not a Spiritist, because they believe the soul came from God, whereas he believes otherwise; a statement which shows Spiritism in a favourable light.

Sir Oliver Lodge, in a striking passage, widely quoted, and of great beauty, even if of little accuracy, suggests that "the wall between the two worlds is getting thin in places; and that we now begin to hear sounds from the other side."

Surely these "sounds" have been heard by man from the earliest ages, and are recorded throughout the Bible, as well as in history.

The general belief now seems to be, not that the wall is thinning, but that the wall between the two worlds for the last few hundred years is certainly thicker than in the early days of human history, when intercourse between the two sides seemed easier. That Spiritism has really "thinned the wall" is still rather doubtful. Something must be allowed, however, to enthusiasts, of which Sir Oliver Lodge is certainly one.

True Spiritualism

Consider for one moment, in contrast to Modern Spiritism, what I venture to call the true Spiritualism of the Christian and of Scripture. There is no scientist or philosopher but can discern the moral difference of the two atmospheres, to say nothing of the certainty and clearness of the statements of the one and the almost unintelligible mysticism of the other.

Many think it very unfair for those who believe in a spiritual world and in future existence to reject Spiritism; but the two are in no way linked together, and the spiritual and future existence of man, as described in Spiritist teaching, is, in nearly every detail, in direct contradiction to Scripture. To Spiritism, survival after death is a theory to be proved; to Spiritualism, it is a fact to be believed.

It will be observed that throughout this work I have reserved the word "Spiritism" for the modern cult, and "Spiritualism" for those mysteries of the

Unseen that are revealed to us in Scripture. It may be that by this and similar usage the two expressions will gradually become so distinct that the one will mean almost the reverse of the other.

True and False Gnosis

The two, indeed, constitute largely the false and true "$\gamma\nu\omega\sigma\iota\varsigma$": of which, in early days, the Gnostic heresy was the exponent of the former, and Christianity of the latter. The gospel of St. John was undoubtedly written partly to combat the former.

It requires no extreme stretch of imagination to see much in Spiritism that recalls the tenets of Gnosticism; far easier, indeed, than to see what it has in common with Christianity.

Sir A. Conan Doyle, who arduously endeavours to link Spiritism with, at any rate, some fragments of Christianity, says that the early Church was saturated with Spiritism. If he means the very early Church, it was with the true Spiritualism that it was saturated; if he means that of even one or two centuries later, it is true, for it soon fell into all sorts of heresies. The Christian faith is not founded, however, on the early Church, but on the Bible.* Spiritualism, as I use the word, is then the essence and doctrine of Scripture, of Christian philosophy, and of truth. In his book he also says, in his new *rôle* of apostle of "The New Revelation," that "no religion upon earth has

---

* It is useless to say that it was the early Church that gave Christians their Bible. It is simply not true. It was given by God alone, and our Bible was everywhere already circulating as the Word of God amongst Christians when the early Church ratified their decision by its authority.

any advantage over another, but that character and refinement are everything. Every form may have a purpose for somebody."

Opposed to this the Rev. F. Fielding Ould, a Spiritist, says: "No one has a right to call himself a Christian unless he believes in the Divinity of Jesus Christ. On the truth of our Lord's Divinity the Church is erected. It is upon that rock that Modern Spiritism is in imminent danger of being shipwrecked. In the Spiritist hymn-book and prayers the name of Jesus is omitted, and the motto of many is 'Every man his own saviour.'"

Sir A. Conan Doyle,* however, believes that the Churches must accept the dogmas of Spiritism or perish.

Spirit and Soul

I have used, largely, the word "psychic" on its current Spiritist usage of "spiritual," which, really and critically, it does not connote at all.

One of the great defects of Spiritism scientifically is that it does not adequately, if at all, distinguish between πνευμα (pneuma), *spirit* and ψυχη (psuche), *soul*. It is the latter which may be associated after death with a bodily form (as seen in apparitions). The former is without form, and is that which, in the blessed dead, "departs to be with Christ, which is very far (lit.) better," and which at the resurrection (a fact totally ignored in Spiritism) will be clothed (but *not at death*, as all Spiritists believe) with its spiritual body.

To misuse these two words, then, causes con-

* See *British Weekly* for July, 1919.

fusion in any exact argument. "The word of God" is stated to be "sharper than any two-edged sword," because it *can* (which Spiritism *cannot*) pierce even to the dividing of *psuche* and *pneuma*— of soul and spirit.

These, in Modern Spiritism, seem inextricably confounded.

The New Revelation

Before proceeding definitely to contrast Christianity and Spiritism, it will be, perhaps, best to lay bare a little further the tenets of the latter, for these are not generally known at all, whereas all have a knowledge, more or less clear, of the fundamental and unchanging doctrines of Christianity. Modern Spiritism attractively describes itself as a new revelation: "just as the Christian revelation succeeded the Mosaic, so does the Spiritist succeed the Christian!" We are not told, however, the important point, who in this last "revelation" represents either Moses or the Lord Christ?

I am very sorry that Sir. A. Conan Doyle, whose strenuous efforts to assimilate the new revelation to the old are deserving of some praise, should have permitted himself to speak of the Divine Son as "a broad-minded model, always progressive, and open to new ideas! Full of robust common sense, but (forgive the blasphemy) occasionally losing his temper." One can hardly tell whether the praise or the blasphemy is the more offensive; both are utterly unworthy of Sir A. Conan Doyle.*

* It is a most significant fact that any connection with Spiritism always lowers, in some way or other, and never raises the reputation of a man, however eminent otherwise.

Allan Cardec pointed out, fifty years before, that while the Old Testament was the first law of God, the New Testament was the second in Christ, and Spiritism is now the third revealed law of God. Is this the source of Sir A. Conan Doyle's remarks? To talk of Spiritism as "a law" seems almost more confusing and ridiculous than to think of it as "a revelation."

Change or Perish

Sir A. Conan Doyle says that Christianity must "either change or perish." *There can be no doubt, however, that it is just in proportion as it has changed that it has perished.*

He sees "no justice in a vicarious sacrifice, none!" Nor in "redemption from sin," nor in "cleansing by the blood of the Lamb," when it has become certain that man has not fallen. "There never was any evidence of the fall of man."* "But *if* no fall, what becomes of atonement, redemption, and original sin?" (What, indeed? but the "if" is a big one.)

He further says, "Spiritism is only fatal to one religion." (I wish he would say which he means; it cannot be Christianity, for it is still alive!)

He points out that, *in his opinion*, "Christ has done no more for man than thousands in the war."

All this is pretty bad, and, if true, certainly destructive of Christianity; and yet we read further on, "As Christ said, 'I am not come to destroy the law but to fulfil it,' so Spiritism says, 'I (who is the

---

* Many, however, since the horrible revelations of the late war have come to believe in it again.

ego?) have not come to destroy Christianity but to fulfil it.'" (This, at least, makes it clear Spiritism does not desire to be fatal to it; as the same writer states elsewhere.)

Blood-Shedding Abhorrent

The Rev. W. Stainton Moses, a clergyman of the Church of England, under the influence of Spiritism gives utterance to some remarkable views. He can find no place for redemption or atonement, and declares that the entire concept of blood-shedding is abhorrent to the spirit world. (Which spirit world? Of the good we read, "Worthy art thou . . . for thou wast slain, and did'st purchase unto God with thy blood, men of every tribe, and tongue, and people, and nation."—Rev. v. 9.)

He writes further: "The idea of a good (*sic*) God sacrificing his sinless Son as a propitiation for man is repudiated as monstrous. Man is his own saviour." (Has he forgotten that the "sinless Son" "offered Himself without spot to God.")

The Rev. W. Stainton Moses absolutely denies Hell (not so Swedenborg); it drops out altogether, as an "odious and blasphemous conception" (of the Bible!).

No Vicarious Sacrifice

He is quite clear, not only that no vicarious sacrifice is required, but that no anthropomorphism takes place, "as in our creed" (his creed also).

It is true elsewhere he writes of the multitude and malignity of evil spirits; but there is no Devil. Further, "Far too much stress is laid on Christ's death.

It's no uncommon thing to die for *an idea*" (an idea! To such has he reduced the salvation of man.)

And yet, as we see in some of the beautiful words of "Julia," that the one who becomes as "the angel of light" (2 Cor. xi.) leaves us in Spiritism all the expressions of Christianity, save what is vital.   By degrees the foundation truths of Christianity are discredited, one by one.

Stainton Moses could not ignore the fact that the foundations of Christianity were practically upset by Spiritist teaching.   He was much startled at first by the way the central dogmas were specially attacked; though afterwards, as we have seen, he joined in the attack himself.

Science and Spiritism

Sir Wm. Barrett tries to steer clear of all this.   He says that "psychic research is quite distinct from religion."   This is true if you confine the expression to the S.P.R.   But it is often used for Spiritism, which Sir A. Conan Doyle says "is religion."

The *Sunday Times* for August 10th, 1919, has an earnest article by Mrs. G. C. Miln, a well-known Christian Scientist,* on Science and Spiritism. She hopes and longs for a *rapprochement* between the two, and is apparently quite aware that the gap between them is rapidly widening, now that Sir Wm. Crookes, W. H. F. Myers, Dr. A. Russel Wallace, and others of like calibre, are no longer with us.

* The word "science" is surely inappropriate here, if its work is research and not dogma; neither Spiritism nor Mrs. Eddy's cult are scientific.

No Dogmas in Science

The true reason, however, of the separation is not the loss of these eminent savants, but the persistent efforts of men like Sir A. Conan Doyle, and even Sir Oliver Lodge, to propound dogmas and doctrines, based on Spiritism, which are utterly alien to, and destructive of, any remnant of the true scientific spirit. Once Spiritism becomes really limited, as Sir Wm. Barrett longs, to a department of psychic research, and foreswears dogma of every description, though it would be no nearer Christianity, it would not, at any rate, be stultified in the eyes of scientists, as it is now. It seems to me that Sir A. Conan Doyle's somewhat ambitious attempts to play a leading part in founding a new religion are already reacting disastrously on Spiritism, and I much doubt that the watered Theosophy of "Raymond" will commend it more. All truth is sacred and is of God; and so long as scientists give us facts and not theories, still less dogmas or doctrines, so far are they working in a good cause. Mrs. Miln, in her article, seems wholly unconscious of the real trouble, which is that Sir A. Conan Doyle says that "Spiritism *is* a religion; and Science has nothing to do with religions."

Theosophy

But to return: the Modern Spiritist doctrine of continued progress from sphere to sphere is usually derived, through Theosophy, from the old pagan mysteries. This present life is no longer regarded, as in Scripture, as a stadium in which one runs a race to obtain a prize, but one of the many halting stations on a long, long trail.

Maeterlinck, who is so puzzled and worried by the phenomena, not the doctrines, of Spiritism, seems equally anti-Christian in his beliefs.

He says: "Theosophy is immeasurably superior to that of the barbaric Heaven, and the monstrous Hell of the Christian, where rewards and punishments are for ever meted out to virtues and vices, which are for the most part puerile, unavoidable, or accidental."

"In facing death," he says, "let us lose no time in putting from our minds all that the positive religions have left there." (He does not say what is to take their place.)

After all this, is it any wonder that we find in Galatians v. 20, among the "works of the flesh," "sorcery?"

Sorcery Forbidden

Turning now to the Scriptural denunciation of all attempts to penetrate the mysteries of the other world, further than what is revealed, I think it worth while to record here, for reference, a list of these warnings, which, of course, the somewhat jaded reader may skip if he wishes, as the remainder will still be intelligible without reading them all through.   The principal ones are as follows (I quote throughout from the Revised Version):—

"Thou shalt not suffer a sorceress to live."*— Exod. xxii. 18.

* See further on for comments on this severe enactment, so much abused in early American history.

"Ye shall not . . . use enchantments, nor practise augury."—Lev. xix. 26.

"Turn ye not unto them that have familiar spirits, nor unto the wizards: seek them not out, to be defiled by them: I am the Lord your God."—Lev. xix. 31.

"And the soul that turneth unto them that have familiar spirits, and unto the wizards, to go a whoring after them, I will even set my face against that soul, and will cut him off from among his people."—Lev. xx. 6.

No Mediums Allowed

"A man also or a woman that hath a familiar spirit, or that is a wizard, shall surely be put to death: they shall stone them with stones*; their blood shall be upon them."—Lev. xx. 27.

"There shall not be found with thee any one that maketh his son or his daughter to pass through the fire, one that useth divination, one that practiseth augury; or an enchanter, or a sorcerer, or a charmer, or a consulter with a familiar spirit, or a wizard, or a necromancer. For whosoever doeth these things is an abomination unto the Lord."—Deut. xviii. 10-12.

"For these nations, which thou shalt possess, hearken unto them that practise augury, and unto diviners; but as for thee, the Lord thy God hath not suffered thee so to do."—Deut. xviii. 14.

"And they caused their sons and their daughters

---

* This was not generally, as supposed, a cruel, lingering death. The "first stone" (St. John viii.) was a piece of rock that was thrown to kill or stun the victim at once.

to pass through the fire, and used divinations and enchantments."—2 Kings xvii. 17.

"And he made his son to pass through the fire, and practised augury, and used enchantments, and dealt with them that had familiar spirits, and with wizards; he (Manasseh) wrought much evil in the sight of the Lord, to provoke Him to anger."—2 Kings xxi. 6.

"Moreover, them that had familiar spirits, and the wizards, and the teraphim (household gods), and the idols, and all the abominations that were spied in the land of Judah and in Jerusalem, did Josiah put away."—2 Kings xxiii. 24.

"And I will cut off witchcrafts out of thine hand; and thou shalt have no more soothsayers."—Micah v. 12.

"And I will come near to you in judgment; and I will be a swift witness against the sorcerers."—Mal. iii. 5.

"A certain maid having a spirit of divination met us (Paul and Silas and probably Timothy (Acts xvi. 3)), which brought her masters much gain by soothsaying. The same following after Paul and us cried out, saying, 'These men are servants of the Most High God, which proclaim unto you the way of salvation." And this she did for many days. But Paul, being sore troubled, turned, and said to the spirit, 'I charge thee in the name of Jesus Christ to come out of her.' And it came out that very hour."—Acts xxii. 16. This wonderful drama demands a moment's pause to seek to understand its marvels. Let us try and picture the scene together, and we shall be most richly rewarded.

The Drama at Philippi

Look at the setting of the story. This was the first entry of Christianity into Europe, *the most momentous event in its history!*

Who could discern the mighty importance of the landing of these three obscure travellers? Only two—God and the Prince of Darkness! Mere men were busy with weightier affairs—the gossip of the court at Rome, the rising influence of Greece, and the like; and yet through the power of the message of these three men both Empires were soon to fall beneath the sway of the crucified Nazarene. Paul and Silas (with Timothy) did not seek out the chief men of the place to make the importance of their advent becomingly known; but guided by the Holy Spirit went down to the riverside, the place of prayer, where a stranger, a seller of the world-famed Tyrian purple, whose name (Lydia), enshrined in the divine amber of the Bible, is immortalised, became the first convert to the faith (now threatened by Spiritism) in Europe.

The Prince of Darkness

The Prince of Darkness was an unseen witness of the whole occurrence, and his plans were soon made. Probably the very next day, on their way to the river, his emissary, suitably disguised as an "angel of light," or at any rate as a "minister of righteousness," met them, and gave the apostle a most hearty and unexpected welcome. She evidently knew all about their arrival and their gospel, and the part in the drama she had to play. This ancient Spiritism was, at any rate, far too wise to seek to discredit the Christian gospel, after the fashion of the modern variety.

On the contrary, she lauded it to the skies for days, declaring it to be (as it was) "the way of salvation," and thus posed as another and a greater "Lydia"—the true and the false were side by side.* And yet the apostle was not taken in! (for the spiritual man "discerneth all things" (1 Cor. ii. 15)).

How different in these times! Why nowadays, if the name of God is but so much as heard at a séance, we feel it is all right; while if one of the "soothsayers" got up and lauded the central tenets of the Christian faith after the fashion of this maid, London would ring with the news the next day, as proof positive of the godliness of Modern Spiritism! It is written that the apostle was "sore troubled," and no wonder, with this perplexing masterpiece of the enemy, masquerading before him and undeniably preaching day after day the truth of God!

Paul Discerns the Snare

But "in vain is the net spread in the sight of any bird," and St. Paul, instructed by the Holy Spirit and "discerning all things," like his Master before him (Mark i. 25, 34), refused praise from the unclean source; recognising in a moment the double personality and the case of "possession" before him. He saw clearly the devil that "possessed" this pseudo-evangelist, and said to it, "I charge thee in the name of Jesus Christ to come out of her."

He never addressed one word to the poor victim at all, but spoke to the real power within her. Are

* It will be noted that her name, however, is not immortalised.

not these things written for our instruction? And is there one single soul who reads these lines so blind as not to see the parallel, or so deaf as not to hear the warning?

The result, of course, was many stripes and the prison at Philippi; not forgetting the loosing of all the prisoners' chains, and the conversion of the jailer, and all his house, the first European men who were converted to the new faith.

To continue our list. "But for...sorcerers... their part shall be in the lake that burneth with fire and brimstone, which is the second death."— Rev. xxi. 8.

"Without are dogs, and sorcerers."—Rev. xxii. 15.

The Witch of Endor

The episode of the witch of Endor must also be considered. It is recorded in 1 Sam. xxviii. that Samuel had been dead five years.

The witch of Endor in a cave on the north side of Little Hermon, in the great plain of Esdraelon, was what would now be called a medium accustomed to necromancy, a practice not only forbidden by God, but also by Saul himself;* so that this woman was more or less in hiding.

Saul came and asked for the materialisation of Samuel. At first the form was only seen by the medium; but when the great mantle it wore was described to Saul, he knew at once who it was, because he had seized this very robe years before and torn it on that memorable day, when Samuel de-

* And Saul had put away those that had familiar spirits, and the wizards, out of the land."—1 Sam. xxviii. 3.

clared that in like manner God would tear away
the Kingdom from Saul, a terrible prophecy that
was being then fulfilled at that very moment. Samuel
alludes to the circumstance (a proof of his identity;
for the episode was possibly only known to the two):
"the Lord hath *rent* the kingdom out of thine hand
...this day." He proceeds in the awful words,
"to-morrow shalt thou and thy sons be with me"
(*i.e.*, in Sheol, the place of the dead).

Saul is "sore afraid," not on account of the appearance of Samuel, but because of his words.

False Predictions

Nothing can more clearly show what Modern
Spiritism really is than a careful comparison of the
recorded utterances of the Fedas, Moonstones, Red
feathers, etc., with the wonderful words of Samuel
(verses 16–19). The contrast between the drivel of
the one and the awful majesty of the other is most
impressive. It is true that on occasions Spiritists
have tried solemnly to predict earthquakes and other
things—but these predictions have proved their
lying source by their falsity.

Mr. Stead himself embarked upon his last fatal
voyage with a light heart, for he could not be drowned,
the spirits having revealed to him that his death
would be from some runaway horse in the streets of
a large city! This he told to me.

The Dead Have Spoken

That the dead have been raised on exceptional
occasions, and for definite Divine purposes, may not
be denied. We have the cases of Moses and Elias on

the Mount of Transfiguration. We have those who after the resurrection of Christ (the first-fruits) rose and appeared in the streets of Jerusalem; we have the man who rose when the body of the mighty prophet Elisha touched his form; we have beyond all the calling from the dead of Jairus' daughter, of the young man at Nain, and of Lazarus, by the almighty power of God. Will any one name these in the same breath with the "Katie Kings," the aged aunts, and the absolute frauds of the modern séance? *

I cannot for one moment say that in the providence of God, when in those days His voice spoke through His prophets in a very special way, that on this solemn and unique occasion Samuel did not appear by the power and at the command of God. But it is perfectly clear that the woman *did not expect him;* nor was it by any power of hers that he came, for she herself was full of terror and surprise, and cried out with fear, while Saul was not in the least disturbed by his appearing.

Antichrist

The last case I will refer to is that of the "Antichrist," whose predicted lying wonders so closely resemble many in modern Spiritism that he appears to me a sort of master-medium. It is said of him, "He doeth great signs, that he should even make fire come down out of heaven upon the earth in the sight of men. And he deceiveth them that dwell on

---

* It is not true, as Spiritists say, that Samuel's is the only voice from the dead recorded in Scripture; we are not only told that Moses and Elias talked on the Holy Mount with Christ, but that they spoke of His coming decease at Jerusalem.

the earth by reason of the signs. . . .   And it was given unto him to give breath to it, even the image of the beast; that even the image of the beast should speak" (Rev. xiii. 13–15).   It must not be forgotten that these are "lying" wonders, in other words "fraud," which I fear is almost a "hallmark" of so many modern marvels.

The quiet study of all these Scriptures gives us, in modern parlance, somewhat "furiously to think."

The Monstrous Union

Respecting the sentences of death on the Canaanitish wizards, all given when Israel was about to encounter these in the Promised Land, and practically only in connection with Palestine, it is quite possible that the esoteric reason may be similar to that which elsewhere ordered the extermination of the Canaanites, and long before, for what I believe were similar reasons, that of the entire Adamic race except eight souls.   In a book like this, on another subject, I can only allude to the great mystery of the union of the denizens of the other world with the "daughters of men," which apparently not only occasioned the Noachian deluge, but the extermination of the Canaanites, for the disaster was not confined to the days of Noah.*   The results of the unnatural marriages were giants† of superhuman powers; and thus the corruption of the whole of

* The Nephilim (giants) were the result of the horrible union, and also, on a later occasion, in Canaan: "There we saw the Nephilim, the sons of Anak" (Numb. xiii. 33), for Genesis vi. tells us "the Nephilim were in those days, *and also after those days*."

† The demigods of Greek mythology were evidently distorted reminiscences of this terrible time.

humanity was imminent. The terrible nature of the danger may be measured by the steps taken to stop it, and the reality of it will be realised by reading the well-known "Giant Cities of Bashan," by Porter, a sober record of unheard-of marvels, which at once silences all scoffers and sceptics. That under these special circumstances no communications with the unseen world should be allowed was absolutely essential to the preservation of the human race, which was probably only saved by an action which has been loudly condemned by ignorant humanitarians and arm-chair critics.

Sons of Anak

Degenerate survivors of the great disaster, however, may exist even to this day. Those who know Palestine are aware that some of the fellaheen are the original Canaanites of the days of Joshua; and in the Lebanon Hospital for Mental Diseases, near Beyrout, to me the most wonderful Christian work in the Near East (and the only one carried on by England throughout the Great War), I have seen one of the "sons of Anak" with the twenty-four fingers and toes, and giant stature, that still distinguishes the once hybrid race; at any rate, in the belief of the people.

Of course, in modern times, this special reason for condemning necromancy no longer exists, though the danger of tampering with the secrets of the other world is still a great reality and furnishes another reason of nearly equal weight. The tone of the New Testament, probably from the above facts, is different with regard to mediums. It is rather the conflict between what is evil and Satanic and that which is truly good and Divine. The conflict is seen to perfection in the scene at Philippi, and the spiritual man, with the Word of God in his hand, is said to be able to discern between the two—the psychic and the "pneumatic." This book is, indeed, a small endeavour to do the same, for the author regards the psychic side, at any rate, of Modern Spiritism as essentially evil in its origin and tendencies, and Christianity or true Spiritualism, as of God, and tending only to the good of humanity.

Wisdom of Jewish Prophets

Sir Wm. Barrett, referring to our subject, says, most aptly, "The ground of the Jewish prophets was most wise; but in the New Testament the warnings are somewhat different: 'Try the spirits,' not turn a deaf ear. The spirits seem mainly psychic; that of the Kingdom of God is truly spiritual, and modern spiritism is mainly psychic, true spiritualism is really spiritual. Every thoughtful and reverent mind must admit the peril to faith in a risen Lord; and there is a destined warning against making a religion of spiritism."*

"To study psychical phenomena," he continues, "as a branch of science is another matter."

Communication with the spirit-world may be with good or bad spirits. Christianity fosters all communication with the supreme good—the Holy Spirit of God. The evil are what are specially forbidden—"Beware of seducing spirits."

* "On the Threshold of the Unseen," p. 34.

Of course, the very forbidding of necromancy shows it existed; but *does not prove it was successful*.

The ancient practice was essentially devilish, and, as we have seen, to be repressed at all costs. Not for nothing has the Christian Church throughout her history forbidden the practice of necromancy. Will any apologist deny it has a most unpleasant and deterring record?

Borrowed Plumes

Spiritism speaks deceptively at times in language borrowed from Christianity: "The grand figure of the Crucifixion will endure throughout the ages," but it proceeds, "The true atonement is the ennobling of the nature, the pacifying of the spirit, the making at one the human and Divine." The new religion will have but one confession, "Love and faith, and Our Father which art in Heaven." It is evident that Modern Spiritism and the true Spiritualism of Christianity have little in common.

Neither the atonement nor the resurrection are accepted by Spiritism. That Christ is now alive in the other world with myriads of the living host of Heaven, as well as with the spirits of the dead, is absolutely unknown to it.

Sir Oliver Lodge beautifully says in "Raymond," "Christ's advent is the glory, his reception the shame of the human race," but he does not point out that that shame has been turned by God into glory on the Cross, and into the redemption of the world; for salvation is to be found in the Cross, not in the cradle, of the Lord Jesus Christ. The language and practice of Spiritism is, indeed, at the opposite pole to Christianity.

Not that it always so represents itself. It is rather, it says at times, an effort to change Christianity, to save it from perishing; and unfortunately it appeals to ignorant masses, already alienated from it, not by their reason or as the result of examination, but from apathy and indifference.

The Child of Theosophy

It was when faith thus declined that the whole problem of the future life became insoluble, and was left to the necromancers of Modern Spiritism.

It is to contend against this state of things this book has been written. It is, indeed, time that some attempt should be made to put this new religion in its true light; and that it should be revealed as a child of Theosophy and not of Christianity.

It is possible Theosophists may repudiate their offspring; but none can read "Raymond" and other books without coming to the same conclusion.

To compare small things with great, we may therefore venture to think that even this puny effort may be a faint reflection of the great conflict of the powers of darkness and light. "For our wrestling is not against flesh and blood, but against the principalities, against the powers, against the world-rulers of this darkness, against the spiritual tests of wickedness."—Eph. vi. 12.

The "Nineteenth Century"

I will close with a few words from an abler pen than mine—Mr. C. E. Hudson, in the *Nineteenth Century* (May, 1919).

"What are the futile and valueless vapourings of F. W. H. Myers or "Raymond" (Sir Oliver Lodge), when weighed in the balance against that fellowship of universal prayer which the Christian knows himself to share with the whole company of the Church in Paradise in Heaven; that fellowship made effectual not through "Feda" or "Moonstone," or "Dr. Phinuit" (to name most celebrated "controls"), but through Jesus Christ our Lord?

"Spiritism has no message for the sinner; the one bowed down in the consciousness of his own weakness and shame. It provides no answer to the eternal queries of the human soul—'Who will deliver me from this body of death?' 'What shall I do to be saved?'

"Where in Spiritism is there any reference to the fundamental Christian doctrine of the reconciliation of man to God by Jesus Christ? Where any recognition of man's *need* of redemption? Where any admission of the Divinity of Christ? It is noteworthy Spiritism invariably speaks of Him as Jesus or Christ, never as 'our Lord.'

"Christianity and Spiritism are, indeed, rival claimants to our allegiance, and there can surely be no doubt as to which of the two has the better right to it.

"After all, what is there in Spiritism which is not already familiar knowledge to the most insignificant disciple of Jesus Christ?"

CHAPTER XIII

TRUE SPIRITUALISM

A Nasty Sound

I GRANT that, as applied to Christianity, "Spiritualism" has a nasty sound, but I venture to say that it is truly descriptive of it. Christianity is an essentially spiritual religion. Its Head is now in the spirit world; its God is a Spirit; the Holy Spirit is the Comforter, the Inspirer, the Guide of every Christian, and the power of his new life. It is, therefore, a great pity that the lovely word "Spiritualism" has been so degraded; but now that "Spiritism" has been invented to describe the Modern Cult, is it too late to restore the other word to its true meaning, and to use it in its Christian connection? I hope not.

Anyhow, whether it be called "True Spiritualism" or "True Christianity," I shall endeavour in this last chapter, which is really rather in the nature of an appendix, to present what I fear is but little known to-day, the true spiritual aspect of the Faith.

The Spiritual Man

The first thing to notice is, that although the "spiritual body," which Sir A. Conan Doyle believes clothes the departed at death, is not put on until the resurrection morning, the Christian is a "spiritual man" now. To contrast good with evil, one may draw a striking parallel, which will not be misunderstood, with "possession." This word describes a man full of an evil spirit, "possessed" by it at the time, with the fearful results I have witnessed. Now the "spiritual man" is "full of the Holy Ghost"; in other words, "possessed" by the Spirit of all good, with the blessed results that follow such a sacred "indwelling."

Let my reader grasp the fact of the existence both of the world of evil spirits, so carefully described in Eph. vi. 12, and of the Holy Spirit as dwelling in a man (Rom. viii. 9).

The "spiritual man," so indwelt, becomes a man of power; according to 1 Cor. ii.: "He that is 'spiritual' judges (or discerns) all things; and he himself is judged (discerned) of no man."

Discerns All Things

The wonderful sight of this power in actual operation demonstrates the practical power, wisdom, and sound judgment that such a condition alone confers, and is well shown in the wonderful drama at Philippi recorded in Chapter XII.

Would that such dramas were more common now!

It would obviously be too grotesque to describe Spiritism as a rival to Christianity, were it not for the rarity of truly "spiritual men" to-day!

It is as such that humanity becomes truly noble, as the spiritual man "discerns all things." It is only the great who, by this power, have any concept how small they really are.

True Perspective

It is a great thing when dealing, as we are, with God and man, the Infinite and the finite, to be able as it were to get outside of our personality and consider it abstractedly. "What is man, that Thou art mindful of him?" He lives in time and space, and only in the smallest fraction of either. One may express it thus. If time be as a year, he knows less than one single hour, as shown in his perception of vibrations; if space be as a thousand miles, he knows less than an inch, as shown in his being shut up in one small planet of the universe. His limitations are everywhere, and the smell of the red earth of the garden where Adam was first placed, but to which his spirit never belonged, still clings to him, and proves the lowly origin of his loftiest aspirations.

None of these things are seen or realised in their true light until his personality (in the new birth) becomes so pervaded by the eternal Spirit, through the power of the crucified Redeemer, that he then dwells in eternity. It is thus that he gets, for the first time, the true perspective of life.

To the time-dweller, *tout lasse*, *tout casse*, *tout passe*. Modern Spiritism will soon have had its day, break up, and cease to be "modern"; for the world itself grows old. Only that which is not "of the world," but of God, ages not: and Christianity is as new and fresh to-day as when its millenniums first began.*

* This is most strikingly evident to-day in Asia, Africa, and any islands of the sea.

Apotheosis of Man

What an apotheosis of man is here. No Spiritism, no Modernism, no Science (Christian or otherwise) has ever pictured, or has ever conceived, the glorious destiny reserved for him in the counsels of God. Purblind bats, as we are, to turn our backs on the grace of a God who "will have all men to be saved, and come to a knowledge of the truth," that He may raise them, even now, up to Heaven; and there, in spirit, in eternity with Christ, survey the incredible destiny of man, who is destined to display throughout eternity to the created universe the wisdom and the love of the Divine (Eph. ii. 6, and iii. 10, 18, 19). "For eye hath not seen, ear hath not heard, neither hath it entered into the heart of man to conceive, the things which God hath prepared for them that love Him; but God hath revealed them unto us by His Spirit" (1 Cor. ii. 9).

Man's Pitiful Pride

Talk of super-men, of the dreary outlook of "Raymond's" other world, of the seven spheres of Theosophy, of the dreams of visionaries! Their concepts, one and all, are necessarily bounded by the capacity of the minds that conceived them.

It is thus that man, rejecting in his pitiful pride the doctrine of the Fall, which somewhat lowers him in his own eyes, turns his back with cold indifference on God's Divine love that would not spare His Son, that men might be for ever rescued from "sin and all its woe," and enjoy through His grace the dazzling future He has offered to mankind.*

What is the use even of seeing the futility of Spiritism, and of being delivered from its toils, if we still are so blind and deaf to our own interests as not to believe the word of Christ Jesus? Once we enroll ourselves under the banner of the Cross we find ourselves rich "beyond all the dreams of avarice," and the much-dreaded darkness of the future is replaced by the radiance of an eternity of joy!†

Christianity Always First

Let a man sit down and count the cost of rejecting Christianity, supposing it for a moment to be (as it is) a true belief, and he will be appalled at his folly. Let a man even take everything for the moment as equally true—Christianity, Theosophy, Christian Science, Modernism, and Spiritism, listen to all they respectively offer to man, and make his choice—Christianity will then be necessarily first, all the time. And when he inquires for the respective guarantees behind Christianity, Theosophy, Christian Science, Modernism, and Spiritism, for the fulfilment of their promises, he will find that the only one that can produce, even a professed Divine assurance of their fulfilment, is the Christian faith.

And lastly, if he asks for the evidence of the

* We can effect no surprise that the apostle should exclaim: "How shall we escape if we neglect *so great* salvation?"

† For years, during its construction, the Simplon Tunnel was but a gloomy cavern; it is now the entrance to the sunshine and glories of Italy. It is in like manner the resurrection of Christ has transformed death from being the gloomy end of all our hopes into the portal of Divine sunshine and endless bliss!

truth of Christianity, Theosophy, Christian Science, Modernism, and Spiritism, in the history of their converts, he will find that the only faith that has, as yet, any history at all demonstrates in the lives of its followers, the world over, its Divine power.

Transforming Power

The darker the setting, the more wonderful the transformation; for there is not one dark spot on this earth, the world over, which the word of God and the faith of Christ have entered, that has not had its darkness changed into light.

Let Theosophy, Christian Science, Modernism, and Spiritism go forth and try the power of their cults to transform the lives of savages and pagans. Spiritism, with which alone we are here immediately concerned, is at home already in these dark places and needs no introduction. Its power for transformation, however, is still to seek. But this is not all, for the half has not yet been told. I can assure my dubious reader that it is not true, as he has no doubt been assured more than once, that Christianity is really "a scheme for making him miserable now, that he may be happy hereafter." It is happiness here and now that it offers.

Now all of us, Jews, Turks and infidels, atheists, believers, unbelievers, and ordinary people, are after the same thing throughout life—happiness; the point is—Who gets it?

Pursuit of Happiness

The richest and wisest man on earth once started on this quest, and spared nothing in order to succeed.

His record is in Eccles. ii., and his name is Solomon, and his conclusion is that all he got was only vanity and vexation of spirit.

One would think that, when he failed, it would be difficult for "a mere man" to succeed.

The fact is the world is on a vain pursuit, deluded by a false proverb, "A bird in the hand is worth two in the bush." This is a colossal lie, and belief in it is even now leading mankind to destruction. Let anyone catch a nightingale or even a thrush, and try if the proverb be true. He will soon be a sadder but a wiser man, for he will discover a great truth. Only "in the bush" does the bird sing, which is all its value; once in the hand, the song is gone. It is true he can eat the bird, but will any one tell me that a roasted nightingale is worth two living ones "in a bush"? The rubbish of the saying is laid bare, and yet it is this delusion that leads men astray.

The Prodigal Son

Take the story of the prodigal son as an illustration of the drama of mankind. The prodigal, doubtless, being properly instructed in error, had always understood that "a bird in the hand *was* worth two in the bush"; and hearing the syren songs in the "bush" of the "far country" (it's always a long journey), he sets out to prove the truth of his lying proverb. He is soon disillusioned, and discovers, as do all men, sooner or later, that happiness consists in the pursuit, not in the attainment of the object. Once possessed, the song that lured us on is silent, and happiness is yet to seek. Such, indeed, is the matchless moral of the "Blue Bird"*—that true drama of life.

Happiness Above the Sun

Men are everywhere striving after a happiness they never get, because of one futile mistake. They are seeking it "beneath the sun," whereas the wisest man assures them "all is vanity and vexation of spirit" there! Why not, then, seek happiness above the sun?

Man is comparatively happy so long as he hasn't got his happiness, and it is still singing its deceptive songs in his ears, because he believes he is going to get it.

It is when he does get it that he really becomes truly wretched. What a strange paradox? Is there any prospect more terrible than that before a disillusioned man—the *blasé* man who has caught all his "birds" only to find that he has been fooled by a lying proverb. He has lost his life, his soul, his chance of happiness, both here and hereafter, because he preferred a lie of man to the truth of God. Why should we not then wake up in time?

I am not writing fiction, but talking from facts before my eyes, as well as from the common experience of men. Believe it or not, these are words of truth and soberness, and probably of vital interest to my reader.

An Unhappy Man

I live in Harley Street, near a great square. A friend came to me the other day and said, "Can you

* M. Maeterlinck.

do nothing to help that poor man who lives in the square?"

"What is the matter with him?" I asked.

"Only that he is the most miserable man I know."

"Why doesn't he seek for happiness, then?" I said.

"That's just what he *has* been doing all his life."

"Then why is he not happy?"

"Simply because he has got all he wants, which seems always fatal to happiness."

He was a poor boy once, but he believed if he was rich he would be happy. He became rich.

He then was sure that if he had a good social position he would be happy. He got it. He then thought that what he wanted to make him happy was a fine, large house. He bought it.

Still seeking happiness, he discovered that what he really wanted was to adorn his walls with the almost priceless pictures of the one artist he adored. He, at last, bought several for a great sum. Still defeated, and growing old, he felt what he yet required to satisfy him was a first-rate *chef* to gratify his fastidious tastes. He got one at a great cost. And now, having caught all his birds, he is the most miserable man my friend knows, for they won't sing.

His mistake is obvious, and is twofold: First, he believed a lie, and was undone. Secondly, he sought his happiness "beneath the sun," where it isn't to be found.

The Truth at Last

Let him, even now, look "above the sun" into the face of Jesus Christ, and he will find there, in the face of His Redeemer, what he has sought in vain so long in the love of himself. The "joy unspeakable and full of glory" will be his at last!

But we haven't done with our prodigal yet. We left him with his birds all caught and in his hand, at the expense, it is true, of wasting all his "substance." Not only his money and time, but his spirit, soul, and body. He is now sent into the fields to feed swine. He opens his hand to look at the birds he has caught, and lo, and behold, they are all changed into the likeness of unclean beasts! He is aghast; he is also starving. For he has "spent all," and got nothing for it, save degradation and destitution. He has pursued in vain all "beneath the sun" that offered him happiness and finds himself now starving by the swine-trough, like many a one in London to-day who has run through life in the same pursuit. "He came to himself"—the truth at last!

This is what men need, "to come to themselves." Let any man, I care not what his belief or disbelief, spend five minutes alone in considering if he has really got the happiness he seeks? If he is, or is not, a contented man? And he will soon be—as the prodigal son was—a man with his eyes opened at last.

Earthly Lie and Heavenly Truth

"I will arise and go to my Father and say unto him, Father I have sinned," he said. And won't you? Here is the path of happiness: for it is in Christ that the Father's love is shown to His erring creatures; and He gave His Son that man might be delivered from this lie of the devil, and at last enjoy happiness where alone it is to be found. For here is the marvel: that very proverb which we have pilloried as a lie becomes a profound truth, once it is applied to things "above the sun." These heavenly singers, when caught, are, indeed, worth not two, but a "hundred" of what they were "in the bush." In heavenly joys only those who have grasped them know what they are. These birds, so far from losing their song when caught, only sing their sweetest when "in the hand." It was when the Queen of Sheba saw the glory of Solomon she discovered "the half had not been told her." Bernard of Cluny, in the dark ages, knew this, for he sang—

> "The love of Jesus, what it is,
> *None but His loved ones know.*"

It is only when the Saviour is grasped by the hand of faith that the heart knows "fullness of joy." Here at last is the contented man! Look at him: the new robe, the ring, the shoes. See him sitting at his father's table in his father's house. Why even outside are heard the sounds of music and dancing; for joy is within. It is only then that he "begins to be merry"; only "begins," for there is no end to that joy!

This is a Sermon

It is thus, and thus alone, that every reader of these pages may himself enter at any moment into the "joy of his Lord." Let him "come to himself"; have done with lies; let him "arise, and go to his Father, and say unto Him, Father, I have sinned."

If this be the result, in one solitary instance, of reading these pages, this last chapter will have done more good than all the book beside.

What's the use of exposing errors, if one is not led into the way of truth?

I fear some may by now have more than a suspicion that they have been listening to a sermon! What does it matter if they have, so long as it does them good? Even sermons have their use sometimes!

A Trinity of Evil

Let me now, in entire change of the subject, transcribe three sentences from 2 Cor. xi, 4, where St. Paul is warning us against the final dangers that will beset the Christian faith. He enumerates three: *"Another Jesus*, whom we did not preach." *"Another spirit*, which ye did not receive." *"Another gospel*, which ye did not accept." These three are with us to-day, and are very fairly represented in our three most popular new religions.

They are called "Christian Science, Spiritism, and Theosophy or Modernism."*

I think we must all agree that in the first stands revealed *"another Jesus*, whom Paul did not preach"; a fallible Jesus, one who shared the errors of "mortal mind," one who served nobody, who did not actually die, and who never rose. A Jesus who did *not*, "come to give His life a ransom for many"—in short, "another Jesus."†

* I see the great Lambeth Congress is considering next year, in a special session, these three Modern Cults.

† It is interesting to note this "science" does not present "another God."

Here To-day

May we not also in the same way discern in Spiritism, at any rate, *"another spirit,"* which the believers at Corinth "did not receive"? The spirit that possesses the mediums and soothsayers of to-day does not even profess to be Divine;* and there is no doubt that it is not.

The analogy of *"another gospel"* with Theosophy or, at any rate, Modernism, as represented by the "New Theology" (which, though perhaps extinct in name, is very active in being), is, indeed, strikingly exact.

We have seen that the coming deception was fore-told nearly two thousand years ago to be "as the serpent beguiled Eve in his craftiness" (2 Cor. xi. 3), and we find on reference to the story that this "beguiling" was by three distinct and lying statements:—

The New Theology

1st. *Hath God said?* that is, "Is there an inspired word?" "Has the voice of God been heard?" In modern parlance, "Is the Bible true?" suggest-ing at once, "It is not; it is no more than any other book"; "we have no inspired word of God," which is, indeed, the first great statement of the New Theology.

2nd. *"Ye shall not surely die."* "Death is not the wages of sin." "Sin shall not be so punished."

---

* Even that blasphemy has I regret to say, on good evidence, been perpetrated by spirits professing to be Christ.

"It is, indeed, a quest after God," and deserves no punishment. Here is the second foundation of the New Theology.

3rd. "*Ye shall be as gods.*" The new birth, as Mr. Campbell has declared, "is when a man knows that he is God." The Divine immanence is a doctrine that is now distorted to prove that the cultivation of one's own "divinity" is the only way of salvation.* A truth is thus distorted into the dangerous lie that was first promulgated by the serpent in Eden.

As Old as Eden

The parallel, and the exact fulfillment of the apostle's predictions, is most striking. We all know that the distinctive features of Modernism, a generic name for the new Theology, are: The Bible is *not* inspired, sin does *not* deserve punishment, and man *is* Divine; and these are the three specific lies of Eden—now revived for the destruction of man. What we may call the "Trinity of Evil" is "another Jesus," "another Spirit," and "another Gospel," as foretold by St. Paul. This is now everywhere around us, and it is, at least, the duty of any who believe in the "same Jesus," in the Holy Spirit, and in the Gospel of God to do what they can to open the eyes of their fellow-men to the activity of the father of lies, who, however, has now succeeded in persuading most men that he does not exist!

---

* Scripture teaches that it is only when man, "dead in trespasses and sins," is saved by Christ that the Holy Spirit dwells in him, which alone constitutes the true Divine immanence.

My Object

My work is done; but I am deeply conscious of its imperfection.

I can only urge that I have sought, in all honesty, from my own knowledge, and from all the sources available, to present a fair picture of Modern Spiritism, both in its creed and practice. Any knowledge I may have of psychology has, I think, helped me to understand the arguments of such men as Thomas Jay Hudson, Myers, Sir William Barrett, and others who have expounded the wonders and mysteries of psychic power, as revealed in the "Unconscious Mind" and elsewhere. These I have faithfully tried to represent in their true *rôle*, as the source, doubtless, of most, but not all, of the wonders of Spiritism.

With regard to the residue, attributed by Spiritists to the agency of the spirits of the departed, I have endeavoured to show that this is, to say the least of it, most improbable, and that a far more likely solution is that they are due to dæmons—some minor form of evil spirits.

As to Necromancy

As to necromancy, one has not hesitated, in view of the denunciations of Scripture, plainly to express one's disapproval; but at the same time I have given what evidence I could, both in favour of and against it. I have also reached the conclusion that, on the whole, no such communication is absolutely proved; while on the other hand, the communications are in too many cases of such a nature that it is eeply dishonouring to our beloved dead to believed that they have come from them. I have not only pointed out the evil, but the good, so far as it exists, in Spiritism; but I have neither disguised nor denied its loudly asserted opposition to Christianity.

While Spiritism cannot for a moment be regarded as a serious rival to Christianity, it is, in my opinion, one of the most dangerous means that are used to catch the unwary.

The Evil Good Men Do

One has only once more to study that marvellous drama at Philippi to appreciate its power for deception, and when such justly honoured names as those of Sir Wm. Crookes, W. H. F. Myers, Sir Oliver Lodge, and Sir A. Conan Doyle are associated with it, and give it the sanction of their support, it is no wonder that lesser men readily follow their lead.* It is only just, however, to add that the first two of the four were solely scientific students of marvels they did not understand, and only two can be regarded as active supporters of the distorted reflection of Theosophy, which constitutes the creed of Spiritism.

I have finally given in brief, a sketch of what True Spiritualism really is, and now I must leave my reader to judge for himself (as indeed all men must do) where the truth lies, and to follow it whole-heartedly.

* It is thus that a really good man may, unconsciously, do much harm.

INDEX

251